D0479699

Start Your Own

BLOGGING BUSINESS

CALGARY PUBLIC LIBRARY

JUN 2014

Additional titles in *Entrepreneur's* Startup Series

Start Your Own

Arts and Crafts Business
Automobile Detailing Business
Bar and Club
Bed and Breakfast
Blogging Business
Business on eBay
Car Wash
Child-Care Service
Cleaning Service
Clothing Store and More
Coaching Business
Coin-Operated Laundry
Construction and Contracting Business
Consulting Business
Day Spa and More
e-Business
Event Planning Business
Executive Recruiting Business
Fashion Accessories Business
Florist Shop and Other Floral Businesses
Food Truck Business
Freelance Writing Business and More
Freight Brokerage Business
Gift Basket Service
Grant-Writing Business
Graphic Design Business
Green Business
Hair Salon and Day Spa
Home Inspection Service
Import/Export Business
Information Marketing Business
Kid-Focused Business
Lawn Care or Landscaping Business
Mail Order Business
Medical Claims Billing Service
Net Services Business
Online Coupon or Daily Deal Business
Online Education Business
Personal Concierge Service
Personal Training Business
Pet Business and More
Pet-Sitting Business and More
Photography Business
Public Relations Business
Restaurant and More
Retail Business and More
Self-Publishing Business
Seminar Production Business
Senior Services Business
Travel Business and More
Tutoring and Test Prep Business
Vending Business
Wedding Consultant Business
Wholesale Distribution Business

Entrepreneur MAGAZINE'S

startup

3RD EDITION

Start Your Own

BLOGGING BUSINESS

Generate Income from Advertisers, Subscribers, Merchandising, and More

Entrepreneur Press and Jason R. Rich

Ep
Entrepreneur
PRESS®

Entrepreneur Press, Publisher
Cover Design: Beth Hansen-Winter
Production and Composition: Eliot House Productions

© 2014 by Entrepreneur Media, Inc.
All rights reserved.
Reproduction or translation of any part of this work beyond that permitted by Section 107 or 108 of the 1976 United States Copyright Act without permission of the copyright owner is unlawful. Requests for permission or further information should be addressed to the Business Products Division, Entrepreneur Media Inc.

This publication is designed to provide accurate and authoritative information in regard to the subject matter covered. It is sold with the understanding that the publisher is not engaged in rendering legal, accounting or other professional services. If legal advice or other expert assistance is required, the services of a competent professional person should be sought.

Library of Congress Cataloging-in-Publication Data

Start your own blogging business / by Entrepreneur Press and Jason R. Rich.—Third edition.

pages cm

ISBN-13: 978-1-59918-521-7 (alk. paper)

ISBN-10: 1-59918-521-0 (alk. paper)

1. Blogs. 2. Electronic commerce. 3. Internet advertising. 4. Website development. I. Rich, Jason. II. McDougall, J. S. Start your own blogging business. III. Entrepreneur Press.

TK5105.8884.M33 2014

070.5'79730681—dc23 2013037979

Printed in the United States of America

18 17 16 15 14 10 9 8 7 6 5 4 3 2 1

Contents

Acknowledgments

Thanks to Ronald Young and Jillian McTigue at Entrepreneur Press, as well as Karen Billipp, for inviting me to work on this project.

Thanks also to all of the bloggers and blogging experts in the blogosphere who have inspired me to write this book, and who have shared their valuable experiences and vast knowledge with me as I was doing my research.

To visit my website, please point your web browser to www.JasonRich.com. If you're an Apple iPhone or iPad user, to access my blog, Jason Rich's Featured App of the Month, visit www.FeaturedAppOfTheMonth.com. You can also find me on Twitter (@JasonRich7).

Preface

You've probably heard all about blogging, vlogging, tweeting, podcasting, and microblogging, but might have assumed that becoming a blogger (someone who writes a blog), vlogger (someone who hosts/produces a video-based blog), and/or a podcaster (someone who produces an audio podcast) is too time consuming, too expensive, and wouldn't benefit you in any way. Well, think again!

In the past, if you wanted to reach a mass audience, it was necessary to land a job as a reporter for a major newspaper or magazine, or become the host of a radio or TV show. Even if you managed to land one of these jobs, you still needed to adhere to the strict editorial guidelines of your bosses, and maintain a high level of journalistic integrity.

Thanks to blogging, however, anyone, from anywhere, has the ability to share their thoughts, ideas, knowledge, opinions, and/or expertise with a potentially vast worldwide audience, and the cost to do this is practically nothing (assuming you have access to the internet).

Using a blog, it's possible to publish almost any type of content and make it available to the world within minutes—not hours, days, weeks, or months. Plus, thanks to the First Amendment, as a blogger, you're free to write or say just about anything, without having it edited or censored in any way. (Of course, slander, copyright infringement, and a few other laws still apply.) But, for the most part, as a blogger, cyberspace is your stage, soapbox, or pulpit, and the millions of web surfers in the world are your potential audience members.

Some people create, publish, and manage a blog just for fun—as a way to share information with or entertain immediate friends and family. However, millions of other people have discovered that blogging is an extremely powerful and cost-effective marketing, promotional, sales, and advertising tool, if used correctly.

Although blogging is still in its relative infancy as a communications medium, it has already changed media forever. Just a few years ago, blogging didn't exist. However, since the concept of blogging was created and started to catch on with the public, it has evolved quickly and continues to evolve at a staggering pace.

Most recently, in addition to traditional text-based blogs, services like YouTube, Vine (a mobile video service), and Vimeo have made vlogging a viable option for just about anyone. Plus, for people who don't want to create lots of entertaining, informative, and original content for a blog or vlog, there's now microblogging. Using a service like Twitter, anyone can create and share short blog entries that are just 140 characters in length. More about microblogging and its potential later.

One of the latest trends in blogging is mobile blogging, which means you can create and publish content from your smartphone, tablet, or wireless internet device, from virtually anywhere at any time. In fact, many blogging apps have been created for Apple's iPhone and iPad, for example, which make full use of the built-in digital camera and video camera within these devices, as well as their ability to create and publish text and/or video and audio content while on the go.

Using the newest blogging technologies, you have the ability to create, publish, manage, and promote a blog, build a vast following, potentially generate revenue from your blog, plus use your blog as an extremely powerful marketing, sales, and advertising tool for yourself, or your product, company, or service. The possibilities and potential are limited only by your creativity and imagination.

Even if you have no company, or a product or service to sell, if you have information or content to share within a blog, there's also the potential to generate revenue from your online presence by building an audience and displaying ads (which you get paid to display) within your blog.

Best of all, creating, publishing, managing, and promoting a blog requires no programming or graphic design skills. You don't even need to know anything about designing web pages. If you can surf the net, chances are you already have the basic skills needed to become a blogger. What you will need is a great idea for a blog, a true understanding of its purpose and its intended audience, and the ability to create original and innovative content.

As you'll discover, companies of all sizes and in all industries are currently using blogs, vlogs, and microblogs effectively in order to inexpensively communicate with their existing customers and clients, find new prospects, and build name or brand recognition.

Meanwhile, individuals are using blogs, vlogs, and microblogs to become famous online personalities; establish and promote themselves as experts in their field; share their knowledge, ideas, or expertise; and to meet new friends from their hometown, their home state, across the country, or around the world.

Today, blogs have become powerful communications tools that are directly influencing consumer trends, politics, journalism, and even the larger national dialogue.

At its most basic level, a blog is nothing more than a text-based digital diary, through which the blogger can create and publish content extremely quickly and inexpensively. A blog can be updated on a continuous basis throughout a day, or updated with new entries (also referred to as posts or content) once per day, week, or month, depending on the blog's purpose, goals, and its intended audience.

In fact, there are many vloggers on YouTube, for example, who are as young as 10, and who consistently have more viewers than top-rated network TV shows, and who are generating $20,000 to $30,000 per month or more in revenues. There are also traditional bloggers who have larger readerships than most major daily newspapers or national magazines.

Even without the backing of a TV network, national magazine, radio station, or major daily newspaper, some bloggers and vloggers are building audiences in the millions, which gives them power and influence, not to mention significant incomes. For example, entertainment gossip blogger Perez Hilton has such a large audience, his opinions and published blog entries directly impact TV show ratings, music sales and downloads, movie box office results, and the overall popularity of Hollywood's biggest celebrities. His audience is larger than the viewership of all the

TV entertainment news shows, such as *Entertainment Tonight* and *Access Hollywood*, combined.

Thanks to the powerful and readily accessible blogging tools and services (some of which will be described within this book), becoming a blogger is a viable option for just about anyone with an idea for content and who has access to the internet. As a result, blogging is being embraced by millions of artists, politicians, business leaders, entrepreneurs, consultants, small-business operators, major corporations, celebrities, housewives, students, and hobbyists. Simply put, blogging is the fastest, most cost-effective, and most powerful form of communication available today.

For example, in lieu of publishing a newsletter, some companies now publish a blog and/or maintain a Twitter feed and Facebook page. As eyes turn away from TV screens, magazines, and newspapers, more people are turning to the internet for their news, entertainment, and information.

In an effort to tap into this vast and ever-growing audience of blog readers and web surfers, advertisers and marketers representing a wide range of companies and industries are discovering innovative ways to use blogging and online social networking to effectively convey information to very targeted or niche audiences.

Once you develop your blog to the point where tens of thousands or even millions of people are following it, potentially lucrative commercial opportunities follow. Blogs by nature have specific subjects that target very specific audiences. Advertisers have recognized this new and exciting opportunity and are sinking vast amounts of cash into blog advertising because it is highly targeted, effective, and entirely measurable.

However, to become a successful blogger, or to use a blog to successfully promote yourself, company, product, or service, you don't necessarily need millions of followers. With just a few hundred or several thousand followers (which is relatively easy to achieve, even on a tight budget), you should be able to generate new business, boost sales, build better relationships with your existing customers, and/or dramatically build your brand awareness with relative ease.

As you'll soon discover, blogging as a revenue-generating business isn't a radical idea. Likewise, using blogging, vlogging, or the various online social networking services (Facebook, Twitter, YouTube, Google+, Instagram, Pinterest, Tumblr, Vimeo, Vine, etc.) as a powerful business tool is something that almost every business, in every industry, now needs to use to remain competitive.

Any publication or media outlet that has an established audience, whether it's print-based, electronic (radio or TV) or digital, can be used to generate revenue in many different ways. This certainly holds true for blogging as well.

This all-new, third edition of *Start Your Own Blogging Business* will help you recognize and capitalize on the immense opportunity that awaits you. Blogging is a viable and accepted form of mass communication. And, due to its low cost of entry, just about anybody can build a profitable business publishing blogs or incorporate a blog into their existing business's online activities.

Before we get started, the main idea you need to take away from this book is that, yes, blogging is easy to do. However, if you build it, they will not necessarily come. Even if you create and publish the most incredible, innovative, creative, imaginative, entertaining, informative, and engaging blog in the history of the internet, if you don't also invest the time and money necessary to promote your blog, it won't generate an audience. After all, thousands of new blogs are created each and every day, and there are millions upon millions of successful (and not-so-successful) blogs already out there in the blogosphere.

If you want your blog to be successful, you'll need to be creative and innovative, target your original content directly to your intended audience, and most important, promote your blog to build and maintain its following.

Thus, the blogging process can be summed up using the following four steps, which we'll explore in detail throughout this book:

1. Create original blog content that's targeted to and will appeal to your intended audience. As you'll discover, your blog can include text, photos, video, active links, graphics, and other multimedia content.
2. Publish your blog, and make it available to the world.
3. Maintain your blog, and keep it updated with new and innovative content on an ongoing basis.
4. Promote your blog on an ongoing basis to establish, and then continuously build and maintain, its audience.

To become a successful blogger doesn't necessarily require a lot of money, but it does require dedication and the investment of time and resources. Unless you aggressively approach each of the four blogging steps just described, your blog will probably fail. If, however, you take the right approach and go into this project with realistic expectations, the possibilities are truly limitless.

Before we really get started learning all about blogging, it's important to understand that these days, a blog can take on many forms. It can be created using just text, or you can combine text with photos, video, audio, computer graphics, and other multimedia content in order to convey your core message or information to your intended audience.

Likewise, a blog does not need to be a stand-alone entity. It can be published as part of a website or Facebook page, for example, or it can be directly linked to everything else you're doing online.

In the past, a blog was mainly text-based. For the purposes of this book and thanks to recent advancements in internet-related technologies, the line between blogging, vlogging, podcasting, website publishing, and being active on services like Facebook and Google+ has blurred. Thus, within this book, we'll touch on how to best utilize many of these technologies and methods for effectively reaching your target audience.

Based on what you're trying to accomplish, you may discover that just using text isn't the best way to communicate your core message, and that also utilizing photos allows you to more effectively reach your audience. Or, you may want to invest in video production (for vlogging) or produce audio-based podcasts to communicate with your intended audience. Each of these communication methods relates to blogging, yet requires a different set of skills to create, plus can have a different impact on your audience.

If your goal is to generate revenue from your blog *and* develop yourself into an online celebrity or internet personality, in addition to reading this book, you'll definitely be interested in reading *Blogging for Fame and Fortune*.

Likewise, if your interest is in vlogging and/or in creating YouTube videos to be used as sales, marketing, promotional, or advertising tools, the book *The Ultimate Guide to YouTube for Business* will be helpful. Both titles have been published by Entrepreneur Press and were also written by Jason R. Rich.

So, let's get started!

1

Planning and Creating Your Blog

First, think carefully about what you want to say and what information you want to communicate via your blog. Make sure you have enough content to share over the long term, and will be able to regularly update your blog with fresh, engaging, and relevant content.

Next, consider who your target audience will be. Then, figure out the best way to convey your information to your audience, and determine if you'll primarily use text, photos, video, audio, computer graphics, and/or other multimedia content.

Think about how much technological knowledge you have, and how much time and money you want to invest in developing and producing your content. Once you've considered all of these important elements, you'll be in a much better position to begin planning and creating what will hopefully become a successful blog. Plus, you'll be able to determine which service you'll use to host your blog, and be able to discover effective ways to promote it.

With thousands of new blogs being published each and every day, plus many being taken offline or simply abandoned in cyberspace, it's impossible to calculate an accurate figure as to the number of blogs that actually exist in the blogosphere at any given moment. That being said, let's take a quick look at how many blogs are hosted by some of the internet's most prominent blog-hosting services as of April 2013:

- Tumblr—191.7 million
- Wordpress.com—65 million
- LiveJournal—62.6 million
- Weebly—12 million
- Blogster—583,000
- Blogger.com—1.2 billion

There are also many more mainstream blogging and online social networking services that host blogs, vlogs, and podcasts, such as Facebook, Twitter, YouTube, Vimeo, Vine, Pinterest, and Instagram, so the actual number of blogs available right now on the internet is well into the multi-billions.

One of the reasons why blogging has become so incredibly popular as a communications medium is because anyone can do it, and the startup costs are minimal. Using a blog, creative and charismatic people are able to bypass the usual corporate content publishers—such as magazines, newspapers, music record labels, TV networks, and radio stations—and deliver content directly to their audiences via the web.

If you haven't allowed yourself to wander beyond your usual favorite websites, you'll be surprised to find that the number

Stat Fact

According to WordPress.com, it hosts more than 65 million blogs. More than 500,000 new posts are added to these blogs daily, and they're read by more than 329 million people per month. These people generate in excess of 25 billion page views per month.

of online journals, photo albums, music galleries, artist portfolios, and other personal sites have exploded in number. Plus, you can find blogs, vlogs, and podcasts that cover every topic imaginable. As a result, new and original content is flooding the web, which has resulted in a true online renaissance.

This book will help you understand the significance of the blogging phenomenon, and more importantly, show you how people from around the world are using blogging to circumvent commonly accepted publishing procedures, and keep the profits generated from their own work, while also maintaining 100 percent creative control over their content.

The material presented within this book is designed around a five-step process. These steps include:

Step 1: Planning your blog
Step 2: Publishing your blog
Step 3: Managing your blog
Step 4: Promoting your blog
Step 5: Profiting or otherwise benefitting from your blog

Several chapters of this book detail what's involved in each step of the overall blogging process. Keep in mind, these steps are equally important and must be given proper time and consideration. Also, some of the steps required will vary based on

"Engagement" Is All About Getting People Involved with Your Blog

One buzzword that's used often these days is *engagement*. It refers not just to the quality of content that's published online, but also to the level of interaction that the content generates from its audience. For example, a blog would be considered to have a high level of engagement if those who read it also post their own comments and/or share blog posts with their other online friends via Facebook or Twitter.

So, as you're developing your blog and creating content, think in terms of how to make it highly engaging so that you can develop an interactive online community around your content. This will help you retain your existing audience and continuously expand the number of people who read your blog.

the type of blog you plan to create. For example, the steps involved in creating and publishing a text-based blog are different from what's involved in producing a vlog or podcast.

The urge to publish your work can be hard to resist, and once you get started as a blogger, you'll discover the process is fun, rewarding, and also addicting. However, you don't want to rush the process, especially the early planning stages. Once you decide to create a blog, the next step is to come up with an amazing topic to write about—one that will allow you to keep creating new, interesting, engaging, and innovative content (blog entries) on an ongoing basis.

Once you've chosen your topic, it's important to develop an overall goal for your blog. You must truly understand the blog's purpose and what you want to get out of it. At the same time, you need to clearly define your blog's target audience, then develop content that caters specifically to that audience. All this needs to be part of your blog planning process, but more on that later.

As with any business, success is impossible without a solid foundation. Take your time with each and every step. Do your research, and think about the long-term ramifications of everything you do. At the same time, keep considering your overall blogging objectives, and make sure your actions will help you achieve them.

While there's no limit to how much money you can earn running a successful and popular blog, it's important to have realistic expectations. Chances are, you won't become a millionaire, and blogging isn't a get-rich-quick scheme. Truly successful bloggers often use their blog as a way to better communicate with customers and clients, or as a sales and marketing tool for their businesses. It's not created to generate revenue on its own.

If you're creating a blog as a business venture with hopes it will generate profits, this requires a lot of planning and promotion, because you'll need to build and maintain an extremely large and dedicated following for the blog before it will generate any serious revenue.

In fact, self-publishing and self-promoting any type of work can be a bit of a challenge. While it won't cost you a fortune to create and publish a successful blog that generates revenue, it will require that you put in serious work—not just creating, publishing, managing, and promoting the blog, but also overseeing the business side of the online venture as well.

Stat Fact

As of early 2013, more than 60 percent of all businesses maintain some type of blog.

Smart Tip

If you're launching a blog as a standalone business, you'll need to establish your business entity properly from the start. File the appropriate paperwork, set up bank accounts, and lay the foundation for the business's infrastructure accordingly.

Once your blog begins generating revenue, either from your audience or advertisers, you'll need to handle the same business-related tasks as you would for any type of business, such as bookkeeping and paying taxes. In later chapters, we'll focus on specific ways to generate revenue with your blog and how to transform it into a profit-generating venue (as opposed to a nonpaying hobby).

Before you start calculating all the riches you'll be earning as a blogger, let's spend a few minutes exploring what a blog, vlog, podcast, and microblog actually are. After all, you need to determine if this is what you want to do, what approach you want to take, and whether you have the wherewithal to do it right.

What Is a Blog?

The term "blog" comes from combining the words "web" and "log," which was used for a short time to describe websites that published a running archive of dated entries, sort of like a digital diary that was displayed in chronological order. The techno-geeks that created the first "web logs" coined the term "weblog," which ultimately evolved into the term "blog."

The word "blog," as a noun, can describe a regularly updated, primarily text-based website with individual, dated posts that are displayed chronologically. This is a traditional blog. Of course, today's traditional blogs can also incorporate photos, videos, audio, and graphics, but they're primarily text-based, and use a standard format for each entry.

The word can also be used as a verb, as in "to blog," meaning to actively submit posts to a website, which is also referred to as "blogging." The people who run blogs are known as "bloggers," and the whole collection of all the internet's blogs is known as the "blogosphere."

Stat Fact

According to Worldmeters (www.worldometers.info/blogs), the total number of individual blog posts created and published per day is more than 1.8 million.

The anatomy of a traditional, text-based blog is nothing more than a basic website with a bunch of dated entries. All of the blogging services that host blogs allow bloggers to customize the look of their blog, by choosing text colors, fonts, and an overall layout or design. Many use professionally created templates that can be fully customized but that require no programming to use.

Beyond traditional blogs, there are also vlogs, podcasts, and microblogs. A vlog is a collection of videos, recorded and edited by the vlogger. Instead of using text, the vlogger stars in their own videos, and often simply looks into the camera and talks to their audience. You'll find many popular vloggers on YouTube. Some have become popular internet personalities with huge followings.

Thanks to Twitter, and services like Facebook and Google+, millions of people have gotten hooked on microblogging. Instead of writing lots of text for a traditional blog, or recording videos for a vlog, they simply update their microblog feed with ongoing entries which are no longer than 140 characters in length (about one sentence long).

Meanwhile, for people who don't like to write, services like Instagram allow people to upload images and include an optional text-based caption, keywords, and location to a photo.

For obvious reasons, microblogging is the easiest to do and requires the least amount of time and effort. Yet there are microbloggers with millions of followers who use their Twitter feed, for example, to promote their company, products, services, or themselves very successfully.

Many individuals as well as companies often use a combination of online activities to achieve their goals. For example, they'd use a blog to promote a company, product, or service's website, and then use a Twitter feed and/or a Facebook page to promote the blog and/or the website. YouTube videos can also be used to cross-promote a website, blog, Facebook page, and/or Twitter feed. Thus, the same core content and message is repackaged in several ways, across multiple platforms, to reach a broader audience using different forms of media.

For the remainder of this book, blogging will be a catch-all phrase that could include traditional blogging, vlogging, podcasting, and/or microblogging. As you'll discover, the most successful blogs focus on a single topic or have a specific purpose, and their content caters to a specific and well-defined audience. You'll also find as you explore the blogosphere that people from all walks of life start blogs for vastly different reasons and with many different goals in mind.

There are no limits as to what topic can be covered within a blog. You can convey thoughts, ideas, facts, or opinions. You can also offer how-to information, share your expertise, spread gossip, or promote a person, company, product, or service. Some blogs are created just for fun—to make people laugh or to share information with friends and immediate family.

There are also a lot of blogs on the internet that are about the internet. These blogs cover topics such as how to build websites, what technologies to try, and what up-and-coming trends to watch. These bloggers alert their audience to exciting news by keeping a constant finger on the pulse of a particular industry, and provide a valuable service.

Companies from virtually every industry regularly use blogs for a wide range of purposes, including:

- To build brand awareness for a person, product, service, or company
- To distribute company, industry, or product-oriented news and information
- To enhance a company's overall customer service and interaction with clients and customers (as well as prospective ones)
- To offer a forum for providing technical support
- To educate customers (or potential customers) about the company, its products, and/or its services
- To entertain customers or build a community around a brand
- As a powerful marketing, promotional, or public relations tool
- To encourage customers to communicate among themselves about a specific topic (such as a company's product)
- To showcase and compare a specific product with competing products
- To teach people about how to use a product or service, or instruct them on how to acquire a new skill

The possibilities are truly limitless, whether you're blogging, vlogging, podcasting, or microblogging.

Not all blogs provide a valuable service. There are plenty of blogs out there that feature content that's totally incoherent, rambles, and features un-entertaining rants about whatever is on the blogger's mind. In fact, as you start reading blogs, you'll find many where the blogger actually blogs about not having anything to blog about.

This meaningless type of blog has no audience beyond the blogger's immediate friends, co-workers, and relatives (if even those people are interested). You should be certain that your blog, and your chosen

> **Beware!**
> A blog can be about anything, but to be successful, a blog must provide a valuable and tangible service or benefit to its readers. The content you create needs to be informative, entertaining, unique, creative, and/or engaging—something people want to read or watch. It also needs to be consistent. Blogs that aren't well focused find it very difficult to find and then retain an audience.

topic, provide valuable and informative content. After all, if you're able to provide valuable and reliable content of any kind, you'll develop an audience, and that audience can keep growing.

Blogging is a fast-growing phenomenon. As blogging becomes even more mainstream and widespread, so does your potential audience. Blogs can be accessed from a desktop or notebook computer, any wireless internet device, an interactive TV set, a tablet (such as the iPad), or even a smartphone. So as more individuals, companies, and organizations use blogs to communicate, more people will devote their time to reading blogs, listening to podcasts, and watching vlogs that interest them.

Without a doubt, blogging will continue to become more popular and evolve in the next few years. It's not too late to jump on the bandwagon and become a successful blogger, podcaster, or vlogger. Even if you can't come up with something truly unique to blog about, you can still develop a new twist to present your content and take a new approach when it comes to presenting it to your targeted audience.

With your enthusiasm to explore the world of professional blogging, and the tools and information provided in the following chapters, you'll potentially be able to earn money running a blog. The amount of money you earn will be up to you.

Keep in mind, many companies currently use a blog as a sales, marketing, promotional, or advertising tool, and/or to enhance their customer service or technical support. The blog is not designed to directly generate revenue, but it is designed to help a company grow, cut costs, and assist in building lasting relationships with potential and existing customers or clients, for example.

It All Starts with a Great Idea

As you already know, one of the first steps for launching a successful blog is the planning phase. Just as you wouldn't launch a company without a detailed business plan, you don't want to simply create a blog without a plan, especially if you're hoping to generate revenue from it or use the blog in conjunction with your existing business.

This section covers the things you'll need to anticipate and the preparations you'll want to make before ever touching your keyboard to create your first blog entry.

A successful blog must have four main features:

1. A steady stream of original, interesting, informative, engaging, and/or entertaining content. The content should be targeted to its audience and displayed or presented in a way that's easy to read and visually appealing.
2. A large and ever-growing audience

3. One or more reliable revenue sources (if the goal of the blog is, in fact, to generate revenue)
4. It should be synergistic with all of your other online activities, including what you do via your website, Facebook page, Twitter feed, and/or YouTube channel, etc.

Choosing a Profitable Topic

There are many factors to consider when selecting a topic that will produce desirable profits or allow you to build a large and dedicated audience. You must consider public interest, your knowledge of the topic, its longevity, and the audience's interest in it. It's also important to look at your competition and develop a way to deliver content that's different, better, and more engaging than your competition. Start off by brainstorming several possible topics you might like to use, then consider the following:

- Who's the audience for the topic? As the blogger, will you be able to cater to that audience and write or produce content in a way the audience will relate to?

A Podcast Allows You to Be Heard

A "podcast" is an audio-based blog. It allows the blogger to record their voice, as well as audio content, and provide it in a blog-like format that people download or stream from the internet and then listen to on demand, as opposed to reading or watching it. Before vlogging became so popular and readily available, thanks to low-cost webcams, YouTube, and high-speed internet connections, podcasting was popular. These days, podcasting is less popular but still a viable way to communicate using audio with an audience.

Think of a podcast as an on-demand radio show that you produce and distribute to your audience. Someone can then listen to a podcast on their computer, tablet, or smartphone, or download the audio file and listen to it at their convenience using a digital music player (such as an iPod).

A podcaster can create new podcasts (audio programs) on a daily, weekly, biweekly, or monthly basis, to which a listener can subscribe for free and then enjoy at their leisure.

- Does the topic have long-term appeal? Will it be relevant in six months, a year, two years, or five years from now?
- How large is the target audience for the topic? How will you reach the intended audience to inform them about your blog?
- Will there be enough to write about the topic in the future? Off the top of your head, can you write down at least 25 things you'd blog about in future entries? Will you be able to come up with new things to blog about and keep your content fresh over the long term?
- How much competition is there based on your topic? Consider other blogs, websites, magazines, newspapers, newsletters, vlogs, TV shows, radio shows, podcasts, YouTube channels, Facebook pages, and other content that's out there and already targeting your audience.
- What will you do differently to make your content more appealing, engaging, entertaining, or interactive?

If your goal is to attract millions of visitors every month to a blog, the topic you select should have mass appeal or be somewhat mainstream, yet have a unique twist to it. As you try to determine the size of your audience, be realistic and develop appropriate expectations. For example, a blog that addresses the political happenings in your town of 30,000 people may very well become the hottest thing in that town, but the audience growth potential has a ceiling. People in other towns, much less in other states or countries, will have little or no interest in your blog.

Even if you create the most incredible blog and the potential audience is the people in your town, realistically, it's likely that only one out of every 10 people in your town will have the time or interest to read blogs in the course of their day, and of those few people, even fewer are most likely interested in local politics. So while the topic of local politics may excite you personally, the reality is that this topic is very limited in terms of its potential audience and ability to grow.

Bloggers just like you have achieved success blogging about a wide range of topics. The following are just a few general areas that you might consider as you choose what you'll blog about.

Blog Topic Idea List

The following list, presented in alphabetical order, is comprised of 101 proven topics you could blog about. However, this list only scratches the surface when it comes to possible topics, themes, issues, or subject matters to blog about.

For every potential blogging topic, you can offer your opinions, experiences, commentary, news, how-to information, or take a variety of different approaches, plus delve into subtopics or related themes. You can also focus on the controversy that surrounds a topic as a way to engage your audience.

1. Abortion (your opinion/commentary)
2. Abuse (drugs, alcohol, mental, physical, etc.)
3. Airline security
4. Art (favorite/least favorite/your review)
5. Books (favorite/least favorite/your review)
6. Boss-related topics
7. Brothers/sisters
8. Business and financial news
9. Cars
10. Cell phones
11. Challenge your audience to do something specific
12. Charity
13. Collectibles
14. Commentary on someone else's blog
15. Company-related sales and promotions
16. Computers
17. Consumer electronics
18. Cooking
19. Corruption
20. Credit cards and loans
21. Crime
22. Currency exchange rates
23. Debate something with your audience
24. Divorce
25. Dreams or nightmares
26. Economic trends
27. Embarrassing moments
28. Family vacations (best or worst)
29. Fashion
30. Fitness
31. Food/nutrition
32. Friends
33. Gambling
34. Gas prices
35. Gay rights or gay marriage
36. Global warming
37. Government/government policies (local, state, or federal)
38. Hairstyling
39. Health insurance (and other types of insurance)
40. Hobbies (golf, fishing, hiking, camping, crafts, knitting, painting, etc.)
41. Hollywood or show-business gossip
42. Home decorating
43. How-to instruction (share your expertise on a topic)
44. Interview people (experts, commentators, celebrities, politicians, etc.)
45. Investing
46. Iran/Iraq/The Middle East
47. Jewelry
48. Knitting/sewing
49. Loss (financial, family member, friend, etc.)

50. Magazine articles (your commentary)
51. Medical issues
52. Mortgages/refinancing
53. Movies or DVDs (favorite/least favorite/your review)
54. Music (favorite/least favorite/your review)
55. News events/news stories
56. Office politics
57. On-the-job experiences
58. Operating a business
59. Parody something
60. Paying off debt
61. Personal experience(s)
62. Personal finances
63. Personal heroes or role models
64. Pets
65. Political commentary
66. Political election
67. Pop culture
68. Problems or dilemmas (personal or work related)
69. Product/service comparisons
70. Product/service customer testimonials
71. Product/service review(s)
72. Raising children or teenagers
73. Random rants about anything… or nothing
74. Reality TV commentary
75. Recent family event
76. Recycling
77. Religion/your religious views
78. Reveal a secret
79. Reviews of books, TV shows, movies, DVDs, etc.
80. School
81. Self-employment
82. Share research on a topic
83. Shopping
84. Single or married life
85. Social networking
86. Something you hate or that makes you angry
87. Sports
88. Teacher or professor (favorite/least favorite)
89. Technology trends
90. Tell jokes/present comedy
91. Terrorism
92. The United States (or any other country)
93. Theatre (favorite/least favorite/your review)
94. Travel
95. Trials (commentary on the legal system)
96. TV shows (favorite/least favorite/your review)
97. U.S. foreign policy
98. War
99. Websites (favorite/least favorite/your review)
100. Weight loss
101. Yourself—share something personal

If you're operating a blog for a company, the blog itself can focus on your company, its philosophies, and/or the people who run the company, for example. The blog can (and should) be targeted to your potential and/or existing customers or clients.

Consider using a company blog to explain how to best use your product or service (i.e., provide step-by-step how-to information), share customer testimonials, offer product comparisons, and/or interact with your customers in an informal way in order to share new information about products/services on the horizon.

> Tip...
>
> **Smart Tip**
>
> If you're at a loss for words but have photos that can tell a story, consider creating a photo blog or using a service like Facebook, Google+, Instagram, or Pinterest to share your digital images. Just as with traditional blogs, there are no rules for creating photo blogs and/or online galleries, so you can opt to include a detailed photo caption for each image, or allow each photo to speak for itself. Photos displayed in a pre-determined sequence, for example, can be used to tell a powerful story. It's also possible to publish exactly where and when each photo was taken, and link keywords or tags to each photo, which make it easier for people to find.

Industry-Oriented Topics

One way to virtually ensure you'll have plenty to blog about, now and in the future, is to focus on a specific industry and blog about that industry as a whole. For example, there's the "entertainment industry," or more specifically, "TV," "music," "movies," or "celebrities." There's also the computer industry, consumer electronics, sports, fashion, mining, transportation, and literally thousands of other potential industries to choose from, provided you have some knowledge about the industry and something to say in your blog.

Within a single industry, there are probably thousands or even tens of thousands or millions of people who work within it. These would be potential audience members for your blog, as would be consumers who benefit from the products or services created by your choice of industries to blog about.

Once you have a general industry or topic, try to narrow it down a bit so the blog will have focus and appeal to a specific group of people. For example, instead of blogging about the entertainment industry, maybe you'll focus on celebrity gossip, or movie, book, or TV reviews, for example. Or you could narrow down things even more, and focus your blog on just sci-fi TV shows, or just a single show/movie franchise, like *Star Trek*, *Iron Man*, or *X-Men*.

The sports industry, for example, would probably be too large of a topic for one person to cover. People interested in NASCAR won't be interested in your bowling postings. However, say basketball is your favorite sport. Consider blogging about the NBA. The NBA has millions of fans, and you could produce great traffic by covering the stories that major media passes over—especially if you have a true passion for basketball and some type of expertise you can share. You could opt to focus on college basketball or even regional high school basketball, based on your interest, knowledge, and blog goals.

Tip...

Smart Tip

Blogs about commodity items, such as digital cameras and consumer electronics, for example, provide good advertising options for bloggers and can potentially offer a stable source of advertising revenue.

If you choose to cover the technology industry, you'll quickly find you have some significant competition. Do some research before you launch your blog. Find out what's out there, and discover a way to do it better, or focus on a different niche to cover. There are plenty of niches within the tech industry, or any industry for that matter, that you can choose from and potentially offer a blog with a unique perspective.

As you consider all of the thousands of different industries out there, you'll certainly be able to find at least one that appeals to you and that you'd have an interest in blogging about. If you choose to blog about an industry, much of your time preparing content (blog entries) will be spent searching for industry news, following industry trends, reporting about industry breakthroughs, and discussing industry gossip, for example.

Blogs Focusing on an Organization

If you have a connection to, or are employed by, a company that holds national interest, such as eBay, Apple, Nike, AT&T, or Honda, you could do well by simply blogging about the antics in your office (providing you don't reveal any company trade secrets or alienate yourself from your superiors and wind up getting fired). People are always interested to hear about the inner workings of the companies that have reached celebrity status in this country. There are many successful blogs run by folks who capitalize on a company's popularity.

Beware!

If you choose a subject matter that's too narrowly focused, you'll have difficulty finding and maintaining an audience, not to mention coming up with things to blog about on an ongoing basis. Likewise, if the blog's topic is too broad, you won't be able to capture an audience, because what you're blogging about won't appeal to a specific group of people.

Beware!

Be careful not to reveal sensitive information, or bad-mouth your co-workers or boss within your blog. Remember, blogs are public. Anyone and everyone instantly has access to whatever you publish. Many people have been fired as a result of posting too much sensitive or negative information within a blog that pertains to their employer or superiors at work.

Within days, sometimes mere hours after you publish a blog post, it often becomes searchable via Google, Yahoo!, and other search engines. Thus, someone can enter a keyword that somehow relates to your blog or most recent post and then stumble upon your blog as a result of using an internet search engine.

Aside from blogging about a company, there are countless organizations, charities, associations, and nonprofit groups that have vast followings that you could potentially blog about.

Personal Blogs Can Generate Huge Followings

Don't discount less specific blog topics, such as humor. Many successful bloggers don't cover one specific topic at all, but rather they cover a variety of topics in an entertaining manner. Think, for example, of Dave Barry's syndicated column. He doesn't restrict his writing to one area of interest. Instead, he writes about anything that flies into his head, but he does so in a unique and humorous way, allowing him to achieve mass appeal. If you're good at making people laugh, go ahead and try your hand at a humor blog. If you can post something that makes people laugh every day, they'll take time out of their day to read your blog and become a loyal follower.

Posting personal artwork, such as drawings, paintings, or photography, has helped some bloggers not only earn money from art sales and related merchandising, but also gain fans and a dedicated following for their work. Thousands of followers or fans gives you, the artist, added credibility and improves your real-world marketability. A popular art blog, for example, can lead to larger licensing, merchandising, or sponsorship deals.

The same is true for musicians, songwriters, writers, poets, and other creative endeavors. By sharing work online through

Tip...

Smart Tip

Once your blog is published, you'll need to promote it to all your social networks. The fastest, easiest, and most cost-effective way to quickly build an audience is to generate positive word-of-mouth about your blog. Encourage your blog's followers to tell their friends about it. Publish a "Share" button or "Share" icons with each blog entry—it's free, easy, and powerful.

a blog, it's possible to build a dedicated fan base or following that can translate into larger audiences at shows, exhibits, concerts, gallery showings, or public readings, for example.

Blog about a Publicity Stunt

Another interesting approach to blogging is to chronicle something remarkable. Think of it as an ongoing publicity stunt. One of the best examples of this is the *Where the Hell Is Matt?* YouTube videos and blog (www.wherethehellismatt.com), an upbeat and heart-warming dance-related series of vlogs and blogs that promote world unity through dance and music. These videos, which are supported by a traditional blog and website, have had more than 50 million views, and generated a blog following in the hundreds of millions. This audience attracted a national sponsorship for Matt's project, which continues to grow and educate people around the world.

Would you like to ride your lawnmower across the nation? Perhaps you would like to try to get a date with a famous celebrity. If this sounds like fun to you, be sure to give yourself a lot of time to ramp up publicity for your stunt before you take off—and start blogging about it every step of the way. Ultimately, you can generate a lot of traffic in the weeks and months leading up to whatever it is you choose to pull off. The thing to consider is what happens after your stunt? How can you continue to grow your blog and cater to the audience you've developed?

Political Blogs

Political blogs of all persuasions exist in abundance across the internet. In addition to entertainment and technology blogs, topics relating to politics are among the most prevalent in the blogosphere. Everybody has an opinion on the matters of the day. Not everybody, however, has an informed and insightful opinion, or an interesting way to communicate their opinions, thoughts, and ideas in a blog format.

If you would like to run a political blog, but not assert your personal opinion, you could consider using your blog as a filter to help readers wade through all the political spin. But, unless you offer something different or unique, there's no reason for people to access your blog and keep returning to it day after day or week after week.

> **Dollar Stretcher**
>
> If you'd like to test the feasibility of a topic before you commit to it, use a free blogging service (such as Blogger.com or Wordpress.com) to minimize your initial financial risk and investment. Post a few blog entries, and see how well it's accepted by your potential audience.

Blogs Based on Hobbies or Special Interests

Many people have achieved incredible success as bloggers simply by choosing a topic they were already passionate about—their hobby. In the blogosphere, you'll find entertaining, informative, gossipy, and how-to blogs about all sorts of hobbies, from fishing and boating to knitting, sewing, collecting, and gardening.

People are also successfully blogging about cooking, home decorating, yoga, travel, reading, photography, painting, music, fashion, shopping, and countless other special interest areas that thousands of millions of other people also have an interest in.

The trick for these types of blogs is to find a niche that you know about and are interested in, and then share your unique knowledge and perspective about that topic. You'll find companies that sell products or services related to your hobby could be your potential advertisers.

> **Dollar Stretcher**
>
> You can create a specialized Facebook page, for free. To do this, visit www.facebook.com/pages/create and then choose what type of page you want to create. You can create a personal Facebook page, or a specialized page for a local business or place; a company, organization, or institution; a brand or product; an artist, band, or public figure; a page that's entertainment-oriented; or that is somehow related to a cause or community. Once you create a Facebook page, you can tap Facebook's vast global audience to attract an audience for your content using a variety of free and fee-based tools offered directly by Facebook.

A Company Blog

As you learned earlier, more than 60 percent of all companies now utilize some type of blog. If your company hasn't yet begun to capitalize on this inexpensive, yet powerful way to communicate with potential and existing customers and clients, chances are, it probably should.

A company blog can be used in conjunction with a website, Facebook page, and/or Twitter feed for example. It can provide a forum to informally share information and be used as a powerful tool to help personify a business.

At the same time, a company blog can be used to disseminate many different types of information, incorporate elements of a newsletter, or be used to help build an interactive community in which customers or clients who read the blog can post comments, ask questions, and interact freely with company executives and/or other customers or clients in a controlled environment.

In addition to sharing news and information about a company through a blog, it can be used effectively to:

- Tell your company's story
- Introduce readers to a company's leaders using interviews, detailed profiles, and photos
- Provide a behind-the-scenes look at the company's operations or a tour of a manufacturing facility
- Share the company's philosophy
- Offer a sneak peek at future products or services
- Provide how-to information about using a company's products/services (supplementing a user's manual or installation guide, for example)
- Compare a company's products to what the competition offers
- Announce exclusive sales or incentives for existing customers
- Tell customers or clients about a contest or promotion
- Allow customers to share testimonials
- Share details about an upcoming event the company will be participating in, or show highlights from recent events, tradeshows, or seminars
- Talk about charities the company is involved with or how it's giving back to the community
- Discuss what the company is doing to be green and remain environmentally friendly
- Answer questions posed by your potential and existing customers or clients

Any information you want to share that doesn't fit into your existing company's website can be shared using a blog. While a website might be written using a more formal writing style and convey a strong sales message, most blogs can and should be written in an informal, conversational style and utilize more of a soft-sell approach with subtle sales messages combined with information, as well as entertaining and/or engaging information the target audience will find useful.

> **Smart Tip**
>
> If you ultimately become a skilled and experienced blogger, you can generate revenue by offering your services to companies on a freelance basis as a blog writer or blog manager.

General Interest Blogs

Don't limit yourself to the topic areas discussed thus far. There are thousands of possibilities that have yet to be explored. You never know what will catch on or spark the interest of millions of people, especially at the wildfire pace that word-of-mouth can travel across the internet. If you have a crazy idea that might just work, go ahead and give it a shot.

Continuous Stream of Content

When choosing what to blog about, remember to choose an overall topic that won't dry up. Public interest is fickle and rarely stays on one topic for very long. So be sure to choose a topic that has held public interest (or the interest of your target audience) for a long time and will continue to do so in the future.

For example, the Winter Olympics is an event that sends the whole world rushing to media outlets for the latest news, and a blog seems perfectly suited to provide up-to-the-minute updates and compelling stories about the competitors. But what do you cover after the closing ceremonies, and then for the next three years? Your blog could easily sit dormant and unprofitable when the public's interest moves on.

No one can control public interest. People can only influence public interest and trends, both of which can be somewhat predictable. Examine trends in the past, stick to reliable topics, and don't select a subject so esoteric that you limit your audience as you choose the focus on your blog.

As you develop your content, keep in mind that the attention span of your audience is very short. For text-based blogs, keep your postings short. Likewise, a video published within a blog or on YouTube, for example, should be kept to between three and five minutes in length.

> Tip...
>
> **Smart Tip**
>
> When creating content for a traditional blog, also keep your readers' short attention spans in mind. Get your main points or message across in five minutes or less.

If you have a topic that requires a vast amount of text or a long video to explain, for example, consider dividing up that content into a series of short blog posts or videos.

Your Credibility as a Blogger

You must have, or develop, a better-than-average familiarity with your chosen topic if you want readers to take you seriously. Readers won't stick around to read things they already know or that they deem irrelevant or uninteresting.

Therefore, you shouldn't choose a topic that you know little or nothing about. Chances are, if you know nothing about the topic you select now, you don't have too much interest in the subject. Ideally, you want to be absolutely passionate about whatever it is you blog about since that passion will come across to your audience. Plus, in the weeks and months to come, if you have a passion for your blogging topic, you'll enjoy the whole blogging process that much more.

If you can't honestly call yourself an expert in the topic you choose, get up to speed quickly by reading books, magazines, newspapers, and other blogs. To establish credibility, you'll want to choose a topic that isn't so large that your expertise doesn't seem plausible.

Few people will ever be considered experts on the gigantic topic of "sports," but it's certainly possible for you to be considered an expert on the NBA. Likewise, it's doubtful that any one person will be considered an expert on "animals." It's more believable that someone is an expert on "training dogs." Choose a topic of manageable size and that can be used to enhance your credibility.

Existing Competition

Before you take on all of your competition in cyberspace, find out who that competition is and how much of it actually exists. You'll do yourself a disservice by entering a topic area that's already chock-full of bloggers, unless you've developed a unique approach.

Similarly, taking on established industry experts can be prohibitively difficult, unless your qualifications are top-notch, and again, you have a different approach to creating your content. You shouldn't completely disregard your chosen topic if you find that it's crowded or well-covered. While that may be what you end up doing, you should consider adjusting your tactics first.

If your preferred topic is crowded, readership for that type of content may already be spread too thin across too many blogs (and other media outlets), thereby leaving all the blogs with little traffic or profit potential.

As you study your competition, take detailed notes in regard to how and where other people are succeeding and where they're falling behind. Learn specifically what works (in terms of your blog topic and its target audience) and improve upon or fix what doesn't. In other words, learn from your competitors' mistakes and don't try to reinvent the wheel.

If you're able to formulate a new approach to a topic or cover it in a new and

> Tip...
>
> **Smart Tip**
>
> The blogosphere may seem crowded on first glance, but every topic has countless unexplored niches. Plus, using your creativity, you can take a different approach to a topic that nobody else has done. Do your homework to find what works best for you, based on your experience, knowledge, passion, interests, and education.

entertaining and/or informative manner, chances are you'll be able to attract sufficient traffic for your blog. And, as you'll learn, with massive traffic comes greater revenue generation potential.

Your Interest and Passion

Before committing yourself to one particular topic, realize that whatever topic you choose will become the focal point of your everyday blogging life. Your interest and passion for the topic should be strong enough to sustain you through the times when you aren't sure you can bring yourself to read another article on the subject, much less write another compelling blog entry.

Consider this carefully and objectively. You don't want to be stuck with a blog you can't stand, and ultimately, a job that you hate or resent. Remember, you're potentially starting a moneymaking blogging "business," which means taking the project beyond where a mere hobbyist would go.

When people read your blog content, it should become immediately obvious that not only are you an expert on the subject matter but you're also passionate about it. At the same time, it's essential that the blog's readers/viewers feel as if you're committed to them and to meeting all of their needs, wants, and interests as they're related to the topic.

Choose the Best Way to Present Your Content

When you're creating a traditional blog, the primary way you'll present your content is through the written word. However, don't forget you can also easily incorporate photos, graphs, charts, illustrations, animated graphics, digital slides, tables, music, audio, video, and other multimedia content in order to get your point across and convey your information.

Choose the method that best caters to your target audience, keeping in mind its attention span is very short. Then, once you choose the best method for communicating what you have to say, focus on the best way to say it. For example, research shows that people love to read top-10 lists as well as bulleted points that break up information into small chunks, making it easier to understand and digest.

That age-old adage that "a picture is worth a thousand words" is certainly true. Instead of wasting several paragraphs describing something, can you convey the same information using a single digital image, chart, or graph?

Deciding how to best communicate information within your blog is where knowing and understanding your audience, as well as creativity, come into play. While it's always good to incorporate one or more photos into a blog post to break up the text, only use images that are directly relevant to your content. Avoid unnecessary distractions that will clutter the screen, and of course, make sure you have permission to use whatever photos or artwork you want to feature within your blog so you don't violate anyone else's copyrights or trademarks.

Create a Posting Schedule and Stick to It

Once you commit to becoming a blogger, figure out how often you'll publish new posts, and promote your schedule to your audience. Then, make sure you stick to that schedule. For example, if your audience expects a new blog posting every Monday at 3:00 P.M. (EST), make sure you always publish your latest posting exactly when promised. Failing to adhere to a regular posting schedule will make it very difficult to build and then retain an audience.

Before committing to a schedule, make sure you have enough content to meet that schedule over the long term. If you publish new postings daily, you don't want to run out of fresh ideas after a few weeks or months.

Even if you publish a new post once every two weeks or once a month, that's fine as long as that's what your audience expects, although frequency and consistency will allow you to grow your audience much faster.

Selecting a Blog Name

Selecting a suitable name for your blog is one of the more creative steps as you get started. Your blog's name should be creative, memorable, intriguing, and quickly summarize what your blog is all about and who it's of interest to. It will be how people find and recognize you.

When naming your blog, there are a few guidelines you should follow. First, create a descriptive name that's appropriate for your blog topic. Let's say a blogger named Alex decides to use the simple name of "Alex's Blog." While this title is accurate, it doesn't give readers any indication as to what Alex's blog is all about or who it's of interest to.

A blog's name should tell readers how they'll benefit from reading or viewing the blog. The title of *Alex's Cute Dog Photo Blog*, for example, makes it clear that Alex's blog offers photos of cute dogs. Readers looking to brighten their day by looking at adorable doggy photos will now know this is the perfect blog for them.

Your blog's name should also potentially work nicely as its URL (domain name), which means it should be easy to spell and intuitive for the visitor. For example, if the blog's title is *Alex's Cute Dog Photo Blog*, some URLs you might consider registering are AlexsCuteDogPhotoBlog.com, CuteDogPhotos.com, or some easy-to-remember derivative of the blog's main title.

Another example is the blog *Jason Rich's Featured App of the Week*. This blog focuses on new and innovative Apple iPhone and iPad apps that can help someone become more productive using their iOS mobile device. The custom URL for this blog is www.FeaturedAppOfTheWeek.com, while the URL assigned to it by WordPress.com is http://featuredappoftheweek.wordpress.com.

> Tip...
>
> **Smart Tip**
>
> Be sure your chosen blog title isn't already in use. This could lead to confusion for your readers and legal problems for you. Do some searches on Google (www.google.com), Technorati (http://technorati.com/blogs/directory), IceRocket (www.icerocket.com), or Blog Search Engine (www.blogsearch-engine.com), for example, to see if your proposed blog title is already being used or somehow infringes on a copyright or trademark. Also, be sure to search YouTube.com.

Domain Name Concerns

Keep your site's domain name in mind when naming your blog. Ideally, your blog's name should be your blog's domain name to keep things simple for your readers. Therefore, you should choose a brief and memorable name that works well with ".com" tagged onto the end of it.

Going back to our previous example, if Alex were to name his site *Alex's Archive of Adorable Puppy Photography*, the sheer length of the name could easily overwhelm the constraints of a suitable domain name.

The URL, www.alexsarchiveofadorablepuppyphotography.com, isn't exactly easy to type, let alone remember. Shortening the name to CuteDogBlog.com would work better. This URL is memorable, brief, easy to spell, and appropriate for the subject matter.

Whatever you end up choosing, expect it to be permanent. Changing the name of your blog down the road will not only confuse your readers and harm your established brand credibility, but it will wreak havoc on any links and backlinks (which will be explained later) you've strewn around the blogosphere.

If readers expect a link will take them to *Alex's Blog*, but they end up at the newly renamed *Cute K-9 Blog*, they'll think an error has occurred and will likely leave your site. Also, search engines will take a while to catch up to the switch, if they manage to at all. It's unlikely that searches for the established *Alex's Blog* will send people to the new *Cute K-9 Blog* without some fancy keyword shenanigans on Alex's part.

> **Smart Tip**
>
> If you choose to go by another name as a blogger, it's always a good idea to create a pseudonym that's memorable. Keep it simple, short, easy to remember, and witty if possible. Also, don't violate anyone else's copyrights or trademarks.

Choosing a Pseudonym

Choosing a pseudonym for yourself isn't necessary, but some bloggers choose to do it, either for the added layer of online protection or for the plain fun of it. Who wouldn't want to create an online alter ego? If you decide to do this, it has its pros and cons. For example, you can say things anonymously. However, by using a fake name or persona, it detracts from your credibility.

The sky's the limit when renaming yourself—just avoid choosing anything that's inappropriate or offensive. You wouldn't want to alienate any potential followers.

There are potential drawbacks to using your real name. First, if you run a blog that feeds off any aspect of your personal life, you run the risk of revealing too much personal information and making yourself vulnerable to identity thieves.

Second, if you write any sort of highly opinionated or "questionable" material, you may be shooting yourself in the foot when applying for your next job, beginning a new relationship, or even applying to schools. It's no secret that people often search the internet for the names of prospective employees, dates, and school applicants. If they come across your blog and read something that concerns them, you could be passed over.

The benefits of keeping your personal and professional blogging career separate could be worth it, but it all depends on your personal goals and your goals for the blog itself.

If you aren't publishing highly opinionated or questionable material on your blog and just seek to provide a valuable, thoughtful service for readers, using your real name is probably a good move, especially if you want to establish or build upon your real-world credibility as an expert in your field.

Write Like a Blogger

Unlike a company website or an annual report, for example, most blogs should be written in an easy-to-read, conversational style that your target audience will understand and relate to. Keep in mind, your blog may be read using a computer, interactive TV set, a tablet, or a smartphone.

> **Smart Tip**
>
> Set up a separate email address for your blog that's different from your personal or existing business email address. This will help guard your personal address from spam, stalkers, and the other security hazards.

In other words, the size of the screen your readers will be using will vary greatly, so plan the layout, design, and content of your blog accordingly.

Here are some basic strategies to incorporate when writing text and creating content for a blog:

- Get right to the point and keep postings short. Remember, the attention span of your audience is very short.
- In your posts, answer questions related to whatever topics you're writing about, including: who, what, where, when, why, and how.
- Use a conversational and friendly tone, but be professional.
- Help to maintain a professional image by proofreading your work carefully before publishing it. Your posts should never contain spelling, punctuation, or grammar errors.
- Use short sentences that do not contain overly complicated words. Always keep your audience in mind, and write using language and vocabulary they'll understand.
- Keep paragraph lengths down to two or three sentences each, and utilize plenty of white space on the screen to avoid clutter and make the content look more presentable.
- Don't overuse different typestyles, like bold, italic, or underlined text. This can be distracting.
- Choose an easy-to-read font and make sure the text appears large enough so it's easy to view on any size screen. Avoid a font size that's smaller than 10 points.
- Make sure the color scheme you use is consistent with your image or brand, and that it too is easy on the eyes and not at all distracting.
- Whenever possible, use photos and graphics to reduce the amount of text in a blog entry and to help tell a story or demonstrate a key point.
- Don't ramble or include too much information within a single blog entry. If necessary, divide a topic into multiple parts.
- Put yourself in your target audience's shoes and make sure the blog content you're creating is interesting, well-organized, entertaining, informative, unique, and engaging.
- Maintain your branding and image. The content you publish as part of your blog should be consistent with everything else you're doing online and in the real world.
- Use bulleted or numbered lists within your posts to quickly convey information. Posts that focus on a Top 3, Top 5, or Top 10 list tend to be popular among audiences.

- Be sure to properly brand your blog using a logo, tag line, and other relevant content.

If you're producing a podcast or vlog, many of the same strategies can be used. In these situations, if you're using background music or sound effects, for example, make sure it's suitable for the content and not distracting. Likewise, be sure your audio or video content offers contact information that makes it easier for your audience to reach you, if applicable.

Again, keep the length of your podcast or vlog short, keeping in mind the short attention span of your target audience. Also, make sure the production quality is good enough to meet or exceed the audience's expectations and maintain your reputation and image.

Strategies for Producing Quality Videos (Vlogs)

When it comes to producing video-based content these days, you'll definitely want to utilize a camera capable of shooting high-definition (HD) quality video and take advantage of a camera that allows you to connect an external microphone so you can capture professional-quality audio. This is particularly important if you're creating video content on behalf of a business that needs to maintain a professional reputation.

As you'll learn by reading the book *Ultimate Guide to YouTube for Business* (by Jason R. Rich/Entrepreneur Press), there is no perfect formula for creating a successful YouTube video or vlog. What works for one company in order to reach a specific audience will not necessarily work for another.

However, if you analyze other successful videos on YouTube, particularly videos produced by your competitors or that target the same audience as you're striving to reach, you'll probably discover some common elements.

Many popular videos produced by small businesses typically have some or all of the following traits and production elements:

- The video is short and to the point. Keep your videos under three minutes in length.
- Within the first few seconds of the video, what the video is about and what it offers is quickly and clearly explained to the viewer.
- The video's call to action is incorporated into the video near the very beginning, and then repeated several times within the video, including near the very end. The call to action begins by stating what the reward is for the viewer who follows through and completes the call to action.

- The video somehow incorporates contact information for the person or organization that created it. This can be done using voiceovers, stated by the people featured within your video, using titles/captions, and/or using annotations or links embedded within the video itself.
- The video is targeted to a very specific audience and has a specific goal or objective.
- The content of the video is somehow unique and tries to set itself apart from the other videos on YouTube.
- The video offers information that the viewer perceives as useful, informative, entertaining, highly engaging, educational, or somehow directly relevant to what they're looking for, want, or need.
- In terms of production quality, the video is professional looking and offers good quality sound.
- The video uses some type of nondistracting background music.
- The video offers clearly defined and easy-to-understand information that the viewer doesn't have to wait too long to receive. The information is not buried in clutter or hidden by eye candy or bells and whistles that can be distracting or confusing to the viewer. For example, animated shot or scene transitions are not overused, and the background music is set at a proper level and is appropriate to the content.
- The look and messaging within the video is consistent with the company's brand and reputation.
- The title of the video is appropriate, descriptive, and directly to the point. When someone sees the video's title, they immediately have a good idea about what they can expect from the video. This is supported by a carefully worded description and accompanied by a carefully selected group of relevant tags and keywords.

With these common traits in mind, as you explore YouTube or vlogging for yourself, you'll easily discover very popular videos that follow none of these suggestions and that offer a truly unique or vastly different approach. Remember, there are no hardcore rules to follow, since video production is a highly creative endeavor. Focus on originality and ways you can communicate your core message as quickly and easily as possible to your intended audience.

Choose the Right Topics to Create Videos About

Once you have a general idea about what your overall goals are for YouTube, you've defined your audience, and have outlined your primary message, it's time to brainstorm ideas for individual videos. Start by determining what you want to say.

Then, based on your video production skills, equipment, and capabilities, consider the very best way to present that content.

For each potential idea you come up with, ask yourself these questions:

- Is my idea consistent with what I'm trying to accomplish on YouTube or with my vlog?
- What is the best approach to take with my idea within the video?
- Will my idea and my intended approach appeal to my intended audience?
- Do I have the skill, knowledge, and proper equipment to produce the video I'm envisioning, and do it well?
- Can the video be produced within my budget, without compromising production quality?
- How do I want the audience to react to the video? What will be the call to action?
- How do I anticipate the audience will actually react to the video?
- Will watching this video entice the viewer to watch other videos already published on my YouTube channel or vlog, to somehow make contact with me or my company, and/or place an order for my product/service, if applicable?
- While someone is watching the video, or immediately after it's over, will they be motivated to click on the "Like" button, give it a good rating, write and post a favorable comment, and/or share the video (or a link to it) with their online friends (via Facebook, Google+, or Twitter, for example)?
- Do the video, its message, its call to action, and its overall approach fit with what I'm already doing for myself or my company elsewhere in cyberspace, using Facebook, Google+, and/or Twitter, for example?

During the entire pre-production phase of the vlog, and then later when engaged in post production for your videos, go back and ask yourself these questions again and again to make sure you're remaining on target.

Why Many Videos Fail to Capture Its Intended Audience

Whether you're vlogging or incorporating short videos into your traditional blog, there are many reasons why videos fail to attract an audience. Some of the more common reasons include:

- They're poorly produced and boring to watch.
- The content of the video is unoriginal and doesn't stand out from the competition.

- It fails to cater to its target audience.
- The content is not entertaining, informative, or perceived as containing any type of valuable information—it does not address any type of work or need.
- It's too long and fails to hold the viewer's attention.
- The content doesn't properly take advantage of the visual aspect of multimedia, so it fails to keep the viewer's attention. If the viewer wants to just listen to content that doesn't utilize visuals, he/she could download or stream a podcast or audiobook, or simply turn on the radio. Consider ways to make your videos visually compelling.
- The video is given a nondescriptive title and has poorly chosen tags associated with it, which makes it hard or impossible to find using YouTube's Search feature or a search engine.
- The video isn't properly promoted after it's published on YouTube.
- Early on, the video receives "dislikes," low ratings, and negative comments, which indicates to those who stumble upon it later that it's not worth watching.
- The producer or "star" of the video has a negative reputation online, which turns potential viewers off to what the video has to say.

Now that you know some of the more common reasons why many videos published on YouTube or the internet fail to attract an audience, you can more easily avoid these pitfalls by taking a different approach when presenting your unique content to your target audience.

As a vlogger, it's often very appealing to simply sit and stand in front of a video camera and start talking. This can be a quick and simple approach to take, but using a single "talking head" shot which consists of a closeup of you looking into the camera will get very boring for the viewer after 10 to 15 seconds. Try to use multiple shooting angles or incorporate some type of movement into your video to avoid overusing a "talking head" shot.

Choosing a Platform for Growth

Now that a few of the intangibles are out of the way, it's time to start planning the logistical aspects of getting your blog up and running. There are countless options when it comes to blog creation and hosting services, and to cover them all in one book isn't plausible, especially since new blogging services and technologies are constantly being introduced.

Let YouTube Host Your Videos . . . There Are Major Benefits

If you're utilizing video within a traditional blog, or vlogging, strongly consider having your videos hosted by YouTube and creating your own YouTube channel for yourself or your business.

There are many benefits to doing this. For example, YouTube offers a wide range of free, online-based tools for branding a YouTube channel and then editing and promoting your videos.

Plus, because YouTube is owned by Google, your video (vlog) can automatically be listed within the Google and YouTube search engines, which are the two most popular search engines in the world. This typically happens within hours (not days or weeks) after a new video is published on YouTube.

Listings for your individual videos within Google and YouTube's search engines will help to dramatically improve the SEO (search engine optimization) for your website, blog, vlogs, and/or videos.

Chapter 2 covers the most popular blogging options, including Blogger.com, WordPress.com, and TypePad.com, plus touches on Twitter.com, Facebook.com, YouTube.com, Tumblr.com, and Instagram.com, for example.

First, let's look at the difference between blogging software and a blog hosting service.

Hosted Blogging Services vs. Installed Server Applications

There are two main types of blogging platforms: hosted services and server applications. Both perform basically the same task of publishing a blog. Chances are, as you get started, any option you choose will meet your needs for creating a basic, straightforward, traditional, text-based blog. However, if you want to add specialized functionality, interactivity, or unique features to your blog, you'll want to pay careful attention to what's offered by each type of service or software product.

There are significant technological differences between hosted blogging services and installed server applications. The method you choose will have a significant impact on how you run your blog in the future, as well as on your operational costs.

If you're not at all techno-savvy, the easiest and fastest way to launch a blog is to use a free blog hosting service, such as Blogger.com, WordPress.com, or even Facebook. When you use one of these services, all of the tools needed are online-based, and absolutely no programming is required. You simply choose a template for your blog and then add the text, photos, video clips, graphics, and/or other multimedia content into your posts using the keyboard or using a drag-and-drop or cut-and-paste interface.

Using a hosted blogging service, you can establish your blog and publish your first blog post in well under an hour (or however long it takes to compose the blog entry). All you need is a computer, tablet, smartphone, or internet-enabled device that has a web browser installed. If you're using a smartphone or tablet, such as an iPhone or iPad, for example, many of the popular blog hosting services (including WordPress.com and Blogger.com) offer free specialized apps that allow you to create and manage your blog with those devices. Thus, you can work on your blog from virtually anywhere.

Hosted Blogging Services

A hosted blogging service is an entirely web-based option for publishing a blog. All aspects of your blog's creation, publishing, and management are done online, using online-based tools. All you need is access to the web from any standard internet browser (or a specialized app on your tablet or smartphone).

All your interactions with the blogging service, including setting up and the posting of new entries to your own blog, is done through the blogging service's website. There's nothing to download or install, no programming is required, and you can begin blogging immediately. This is also a very low-cost option. In fact, many of the hosted blogging services are free of charge.

To first establish your blog, you'll need to choose a blog hosting service, and then register with that service. This process takes no more than a few minutes. To register initially, you'll need to supply basic information about yourself, including your name and email address.

Once registered, you're given a web address URL for your blog. Your blog's address, at least initially, will be some extension of the blogging service's address. Some services allow you to choose this extension, and some assign it to you. Your new blog's address could take any of several different formats.

To make things easy for your followers, ultimately what you'll want to do is register an easy-to-remember domain name, and then forward it to your assigned blog address.

For casual bloggers, the provided address will usually suffice, but you can register your own custom domain name for under $15 per year using a service like GoDaddy (www.godaddy.com). Once you register a domain name, you can forward the registered

URL to any website address, such as the one provided to you by your blog hosting service.

The benefit of using a custom domain name is that you can advertise your own easy-to-remember and more professional domain name, which would automatically redirect visitors to your blog.

For example, when the blog "Jason Rich's Featured App of the Week" was registered with the WordPress.com service, it was assigned the URL http://featuredappoftheweek.wordpress.com. To make things easier for the blog's audience, the URL "www.FeaturedAppOfTheWeek.com" was registered using GoDaddy.com and forwarded to the appropriate place. Now, someone who wants to access this blog can simply enter www.FeaturedAppOfTheWeek into their browser, as opposed to a more complex or confusing URL.

> Tip...
>
> **Smart Tip**
>
> Ultimately, your goal as a blogger should be to get your readers to subscribe to your blog. This way, they can receive automatic emails when you publish new content, or the RSS reader they use will automatically download your blog's content and make it available to the reader without them having to manually visit the blog by entering a URL into their browser each time. The ability to add a "Subscribe" button to your blog is built into many blogging services and platforms, or it can easily be added using a plug-in or widget.

Many of the popular blogging services have multiple levels of service, ranging from a basic, free service to a more expensive, fully featured one. As your blog outgrows the basic level of service, your monthly fees may increase. The good news is the top level of service isn't very expensive (usually less than $30 per month).

For a traditional, text-based blog, a free service is usually more than adequate for most bloggers. At the same time, producing and hosting a podcast is also free, as is creating your own YouTube channel, which can be used to showcase your YouTube videos (vlogs).

In the past, one of the main disadvantages to hosted blogging services was the limited ability to truly customize your blog. These services use prefab templates that a blogger can choose from and then customize. However, with all the recent technologies, the services still rely on templates, but each is extremely customizable from a visual standpoint. The only potential limitation is if you want to add features and functionality to your blog that are unusual or that the service doesn't support.

Many third parties now offer widgets that add functionality to blogs hosted by specific blog hosting services, such as Blogger.com or WordPress.com. While a template provides a design that the blogger can then customize, adding widgets to a blog gives it added functionality, such as the ability to display a slide show, automatically publish news headlines, or adding a "Share" button to a blog entry.

Dollar Stretcher

Most domain name registrars offer a discount on registration fees if you purchase more than one year at a time. If you're sure you would like the selected domain for a while, buy two, three, or four years upfront to save money.

It's also possible to register multiple domain names and have them all forward to the same blog. This can be useful for marketing purposes or to help you promote your blog to specific audiences.

If you use a hosted blogging service and their servers go down for any amount of time, you're left largely without recourse (with the major blogging services, however, this is a very rare occurrence). If you sign on with an established and reputable service, this shouldn't be a large concern for you, as they no doubt have a robust network and highly skilled technicians, plus backups. But if you host your own blogging application or use a separate web host, you could be required to take a more active role in getting the site back online. (This might be more responsibility than you want or need initially, unless you're creating a blog for a well-established company.)

Another potential drawback of hosted blogging services is that your blog will be on a server with thousands of other blogs. If one of those blogs has a huge traffic spike, the server's system resources (memory, processor, bandwidth) could potentially be eaten up by the popular blog, taking resources away from your blog and slowing down service for your readers. Again, if you use one of the major blogging services, this won't be an issue.

When you're shopping for a hosted blogging service, in addition to the concerns already listed, also consider the size and reputation of the service. Don't try to save a few bucks per month by going with a small and unknown service. Stick with names you know and can trust. Blogger.com, for example, is owned and operated by Google.

The main advantages to hosted blogging services are that they're all easy to set up, have a relatively low cost of entry (often free), they provide a nice selection of features, and tech support is readily available. These services also typically offer hundreds of different design templates, plus many widgets you can add to customize the look and functionality of your blog easily—with no programming required.

Smart Tip

Many blogging services offer free or low-cost plans. Try out a few before you select just one. Your time and money will be well-spent. Find blogs you particularly like or that have the look, functionality, and features you want for your blog, and determine what service is used to host each of them.

If you don't have a website design or technical background, and you just want to focus on creating and publishing a blog,

Need More Technical Expertise? Seek Out Professional Help

Installing a blogging application on a web server requires some familiarity with FTP, file permissions, and directory structure. It can be daunting, but not impossible, for those unfamiliar with these concepts to initially set up and then properly run the application.

If you opt to take this route, which is common if your company already hosts a website and you want to add a blog to the existing website, consider hiring a freelance website designer/programmer to help you initially establish and publish the blog. Once it's set up, updating the blog with new posts is always a straightforward process that even a non-tech-savvy person can handle.

You can find and hire a reputable and skilled website designer/programmer from a service like eLance (www.elance.com). This can be done for as little as $200 to $300 to get you started.

using one of the blog services described within Chapter 2, for example, is definitely your best bet.

Installed Server Applications

If you'll be operating a blog on behalf of a company, and you know the blog will receive a significant level of traffic, or if you must have specific features and functionality within the blog that the traditional blog services don't offer, then using an installed server application for your blog is probably the right way to go, assuming you have the knowledge and resources to use it.

An installed server application is a program that you, the user, install on your own web server or web host account. Available blogging server applications range in size and quality from small hobbyist scripts to large commercial applications. There are free, open-source applications, as well as expensive, proprietary ones.

Experiment with the open-source software blogging applications first, as these don't cost anything to use. You'll probably discover that many of them are better quality than their commercial counterparts.

Running your own blogging application allows for infinite control over your blog, its design, and its overall functionality and performance. If you're familiar with the code in which the application was written, there's nothing stopping you from making any changes you deem necessary. Don't let the idea of tinkering in code scare you away from this option; most users never find it necessary because most of these applications are well-polished and easy-to-use. Plus, you can always hire a freelance programmer/website designer from a service such as elance.com to help you customize your blog's programming, if you deem it absolutely necessary. Information about downloading and installing a few of these applications are covered within Chapter 2.

Dollar Stretcher

Using free, open-source software and a low-cost web host offers an inexpensive blog setup that has plenty of room to grow and customize in the future.

The main benefit of using an installed application is that you'll enjoy more control over every aspect of running your blog. The web server will be under your control (either humming along in your basement or through your web hosting provider), as well as the application, advertising integration, and system backups.

One major drawback to this method is that because you have all the control, you also have all of the responsibility. If the server goes down, it will be up to you to fix it (unless you're using a web hosting provider, who can help you with outages). If the blogging application won't load properly, it will be up to you to fix it. And if the advertising doesn't load properly, it will be up to you to make nice with your sponsors . . . and fix it. Again, this option is for people with more technical backgrounds, or who need very specialized functionality in conjunction with their blog.

You'll need to register a domain name if you choose this method of running a blog (it's not an option), and you'll likely need to pay monthly hosting fees, based on storage space and bandwidth requirements. This method may be more expensive in the beginning, but as your blog grows, your expenses will probably not grow with it. So, down the road, as your blog-related advertising or merchandising revenue rises, your profits most likely won't be eaten up by higher service fees.

Suitability for Your Content

When researching the various blogging platforms, be sure to consider your intended content. In terms of storage, functionality, and bandwidth, for example, your needs will be vastly different if you'll be operating a traditional text-based blog versus publishing podcasts or videos.

All the traffic analysis and ad network integration in the world won't help you if the service doesn't allow you to post photos on your photo blog. The first thing to look for in a blogging service or application is the ability to handle the content you wish to include within your blog.

In some cases, a blog is comprised simply of text, hyperlinks, and photos. To meet the needs of this type of blog, any blog service you choose will be able to handle all the content you need. But as the blogging phenomenon has expanded, so have the requirements of the bloggers. To keep up with the competition, you may need your blog to play audio clips, videos, Flash animations, or have some level of interactivity. Be sure to check out the feature lists of each blog platform.

Advertising Capacity

Depending on the goals of your blog, you may choose to generate revenue from it by displaying ads from other companies. Most of the blogging services have built-in advertising capabilities, plus the ability to quickly integrate Google AdSense ads or other forms of display or search advertising ads (which will be explained in Chapter 4).

This functionality makes generating revenue by displaying ads relatively easy, assuming your blog receives significant traffic and the displayed ads interest your blog's audience. Popular ad networks, such as Google's AdSense, sometimes affiliate themselves with a particular blogging service to enable users of that service to install their ads in a few steps.

Once your blog begins drawing serious traffic, you may outgrow Google AdSense advertising, and depending on the blog service you ultimately use, incorporating other outside ad networks may not be allowed or technically possible.

There may come a time in your blogging life when you'll want to solicit individual advertisers and/or belong to multiple ad networks. Therefore, you should find a blogging service that not only makes advertising easy in the beginning but also allows for expansion. Ask the blog service providers if they lock you into a single ad network and if they allow access to your blog's template code for more ad integration later. Advertising integration is covered in more detail within Chapters 2 and 4.

> **Beware!**
> Some blogging services don't allow advertising by bloggers. Don't assume that your ads are allowed. Check first before registering with a blog hosting service.

Future Growth

Blogging trends change quickly and new technologies are constantly being introduced. Thus your needs as a blogger will evolve. For example, when blogs first started to become popular, they were read primarily on computer screens. Today, many people access blogs, podcasts, and vlogs from wireless mobile devices, such as tablets and smartphones. Make sure your blog accommodates these technologies by auto-formatting content on smaller screens, for example.

Plan on the audience for your blog growing over time, which means greater need for storage space and bandwidth. If you choose to use a blog service, it may have traffic and storage maximums—especially for its free services. You may find that as you grow, so will the fees for maintaining your blog, which may or may not be a deciding factor for you. Again, you'll want to consider the purpose of your blog, the functionality you'd like to incorporate, your long-term goals, and your intended audience before choosing a blog hosting service.

At the most basic level for a traditional blog, your blogging service will need to provide archiving, visitor comments, and easy-to-use posting and design tools. Archiving, for example, is a key feature to consider. You'll need the ability to archive all your posts so your readers can access anything you've written since the start of the blog. This archiving should be accessible using keyword searches, posted blog entry listings, and via hyperlinks, for example.

If you choose to host your own blogging software, archiving should be built into any application you choose so that won't be as much of a problem. However, your web host may have traffic and storage restrictions. There are so many web hosts on the internet, finding a cheap and reliable host for your blog shouldn't be too difficult, provided you do your pre-planning and research to determine your needs.

Customization

As your blog grows and you become more familiar with the platform and subject you've chosen, you'll no doubt begin to fine-tune the whole operation for better speed, performance, search engine ratings, and functionality. If you're using a hosted blogging service, the amount of tinkering you're allowed to do may be somewhat limited.

Understandably, if the blogging service wants its service to remain fast and reliable, it can't allow all its customers access to the site's code and allow them to tinker with it. Some sites do allow bloggers access to their blog template source code, which provides for enough customization to satisfy the average blogger. If, however, you're the type of person who likes to bury your hands in the guts of an engine to

> **Beware!**
> Customizing a blog's application code should only be undertaken by those who understand the programming language in which the application was written, and only if the application's user license allows.

squeeze out the last little bit of horsepower, you may not be satisfied with the template customization restrictions imposed by many blogging services. As you do your research, ask about customization.

If you know already that you can't live with customization restrictions, your best bet is to use a blogging application on a separate web hosting account. There are plenty of blogging applications that allow bloggers to tinker to no end. Some make it easy, with intricate configuration menus, and some require diving into the actual code. If you have no familiarity with the code in which the application was written, it's best to keep out of it. Learn the code somewhere else (or hire a programmer), and then, when you're more comfortable with the system, take your shot.

Bringing On Staff or Contributors

Like any business, operating a blog has many responsibilities and tasks involved, above and beyond creating and publishing blog entries and content. In addition to writing or producing the actual blog, you'll need to manage the integrated advertising displayed within the blog (if applicable), handle the blog's marketing and promotion, oversee the blog's business-related accounting and bookkeeping, and manage the business relationships with your hosting service and related vendors.

Sure, blogging is a fun business, but it's still a very real business, and if its goal is to generate an income, it needs to be treated like a serious business (at least behind the scenes). Likewise, if a blog is being used in conjunction with your existing business, it needs to be treated like a business tool—not a hobby.

> Tip...
>
> **Smart Tip**
> Plan to hire help. If you think of your blog as a business, not as a hobby, you should probably plan to have help, at least in the form of freelancers, if not part-time or full-time employees.

As your blog grows, it may become too big of a project for just one person to handle all the required responsibilities. When getting started, your main goal should be to run a reliable blog, while planning the business's structure for growth. You shouldn't assume that you can do everything the business needs for as long as the business needs it.

Depending on your blog's goal and audience, it may need to be updated every single day, or several times throughout the day. Are you planning a life wherein you never get a vacation, or even a weekend off?

Many blogging services offer now the ability to create blog entries and then predetermine exactly when each entry will be published. Thus, if you have a vacation planned, you can write multiple blog entries ahead of time and arrange for them to automatically be posted, one at a time, based on your blog's publishing schedule.

> **Tip...**
>
> **Smart Tip**
>
> Your blog will benefit from a business plan. Sample business plans are available online from the SBA. Visit www.sba.gov for more information. Business Plan Pro from Palo Alto Software (www.businessplanpro.com) is one of the most powerful business plan creation tools on the market. It's priced starting at $99.95 for the basic edition or $159.95 for the "Premiere" edition. This software is well worth the investment if you need to create a detailed, well-organized, and highly professional business plan.

In the beginning, you'll likely be able to do everything yourself. But there may come a point when you simply can't do everything you need to do in the course of the day. In addition to researching and writing posts for your blog, you'll also need to solicit advertisers, manage advertising networks, process merchandise orders, pack and ship orders, e-mail readers, and manage the day-to-day operations of the business, as well as the smooth operation of your blog.

As your business grows, taking care of all the peripheral work that building a successful blog requires also becomes your responsibility. Before you become overwhelmed by the amount of work required to keep your successful blog going (once it has a huge following and is generating revenue for you, if that's its goal), or if you notice that the quality of your posts is beginning to suffer because you're too busy with the "back office" part of your blog business, it is time to hire help.

Unfortunately, many business owners must reach a point of absolute frenzy before they realize the need to hire help. Essentially, in order to take on a full-time employee, the business owner often must overload himself with the work of two (or more) people just to build the venture to the point that it can support another salary. Don't wait for that point if you can avoid it.

Luckily, when just starting out, you likely won't need full-time help. A person or two, for a few hours a week, will significantly lighten your load and allow you to focus on delivering quality content to your readers. Consider hiring college interns or paid freelancers to pick up the slack when their help is needed.

Your Growth Plan

Before you even begin blogging, it's important to have a detailed growth plan. This plan should consist of the short- and long-term goals for your blog and for your overall business, as well as a time frame in which to achieve each goal. You'll also want to determine what type of specialized help you'll need along the way, whether it's from a graphic designer, professional photographer, editor, website designer, programmer, bookkeeper, advertising sales representative, chat room monitor, or an experienced writer/journalist (copywriter).

Business Goals

Specific goals for a blogging business are unique to every blogger. Some prefer to blog in their spare time for extra cash, while others have a full-time career path in mind. Other bloggers aim for world domination. When deciding your goals, take into account the level of intricacy you're prepared to deal with and the amount of time you want to spend. Once again consider your passion for the project and what realistic expectations you have for it.

A small blog with one advertising network is obviously less complicated and time-consuming to deal with than managing a huge blog with private sponsors, three ad networks, and branded T-shirts and coffee mugs for sale.

Many bloggers are able to generate a nice income by selling customized shirts and merchandise based around their blog's name, theme, or subject matter. Just a few of the companies that can help make the creation and selling of merchandise from your blog easier are District Lines (www.districtlines.com), BigCartel (http://bigcartel.com), and CafePress (www.cafepress.com). We'll talk more about this viable method of generating revenue from your blog later.

Your Time Frame

Develop a reasonable and conservative time frame in which you expect to achieve each of your goals. It usually makes sense to take your biggest and most ambitious goals and divide them up into a series of smaller, more achievable goals, each with its own deadline. Achieving five small goals, one at a time, is easier and much less daunting than trying to tackle a single major goal.

If you've planned a modest blog, aim for achieving your desired readership levels in six months to a year, but be sure to keep your expectations realistic, based on your ability to market your blog and who your intended audience will be.

If you've considerably more ambitious goals, achieving your desired level of readership could take anywhere from one to four years. Make sure you have the patience to be persistent and stay on track over the long term, or don't get started at all.

Some blogs catch on with an audience very quickly and require limited marketing and promotion, thanks to overwhelming word-of-mouth or if the blog receives national publicity, for example. But you should not count on that level of success, at least right away. Realistically, it will take considerable time for your readership to grow.

Tip...

Smart Tip

If you haven't reached your goal within two to three years, or your audience has stopped growing for several months in a row, re-evaluate your marketing strategies, your overall approach, and how you've defined your target audience.

Make sure your goals are realistic. When you first launch a blog, it could take weeks or months (possibly years) to build up a significant audience, even if you do everything right from day one.

Inviting Other People to Contribute to Your Blog

You may begin to feel swamped by the responsibility of writing several blog posts per day while at the same time interacting with your blog's readers and followers. If you think that your time would be better spent working on other aspects of the business, consider hiring or enlisting the help of blog contributors.

The best place to find such help is among your readership. The people who visit your blog regularly have already displayed a sincere interest in your content. There are probably a few people in your audience who would love a chance to begin writing for their favorite blog. There's a thrill in being a reader-turned-poster; most readers would jump at the chance to post to the blog, even without pay.

If you're operating a company blog, get your coworkers or company executives involved. For example, have individuals from various departments within your company serve as guest bloggers in order to provide your audience with content that's published from slightly different perspectives.

When choosing a contributor, make sure:

- They're passionate about the blog's topic.
- They're extremely knowledgeable about the blog's topic.
- They're credible and can write with authority.
- They truly understand and identify with your blog's target audience.
- They have the ability to write and edit their own work and create professional quality content.

- They're creative and able to generate content that's original, engaging, and of interest to your target audience.
- They'll work within a budget you can afford to pay. Hiring a professional writer will mean paying them per word or per entry for their work. The quality will most likely be top-notch, but if you want to hire a highly skilled professional writer to contribute to your blog, you'll need to pay wages equivalent to a newspaper, magazine or other media outlets. This often means paying between $.25 and $1 per word.

Beware!

If your audience has come to enjoy your work as a blogger, don't step back from posting entirely, or your business plan could backfire. Be sure to watch the posted material from other writers closely, and act as an editor when necessary.

The drawback to finding volunteer bloggers to contribute to your blog is finding people who are reliable and able to create content that's up to par. Plus, you'll often have a hard time imposing quotas on volunteer help. Asking for daily content from volunteers is requesting a lot. And if you decide that the volunteer you've enlisted is not producing the quality of content that you would like, you'll have a harder time asking that person to stop. Paying contributors even a small stipend makes it easier to set a minimum number of posts per day, and to fire posters that don't produce quality.

Once you start bringing in contributors to your blog, plan to serve as editor-in-chief for any bloggers you hire. You can't take the risk of hiring help without maintaining full editorial control. Your blog could suffer heavily from an incompetent, unreliable, or uninformed blogger. Until you can trust that a certain person will reliably produce worthy content for you, insist that everything he or she posts passes through you first. This will create more work for you in the short term, as you'll be writing your own posts while editing others, but it will pay off in the long run.

If you're able to find several reliable contributors—enough to cover your daily posting duties—you could conceivably get out of posting to your blog altogether and focus on finding more readers, advertisers, and therefore, profits. That is, if that's the part of the blogging business you like best. Of course, you could also hire people to handle these nonblogging-related business activities and focus simply on being a blogger.

> **Smart Tip**
> Most successful blogs somehow utilize Facebook, Twitter, and other online social networking sites as promotional and audience-building tools. Highly targeted paid online advertising can also be used as a quick yet inexpensive way to build an audience. We'll explore these options within Chapter 3.

Don't Forget About Building Your Audience

For the majority of bloggers, the biggest and most time-consuming challenge is building and maintaining an audience. Without an audience that's constantly growing, you won't be able to generate revenue from your blog or achieve any of its other objectives.

So in addition to pre-planning how you'll operate your business and create and publish your blog on an ongoing basis, put a lot of thought and consideration into how you'll market and promote your blog initially and on an ongoing basis. Without an extremely strong, innovative, and well-developed marketing and promotional plan, your blog is almost guaranteed to fail.

Realistically, if you want to have a successful blog, you must become an expert at marketing and promotions and truly understand who your target audience is and how to reach those people with appropriate content starting from day one. Later in this book we'll discuss specific marketing and promotional strategies, but if you're not willing to invest the time, effort, and money to do this properly, you will not be able to generate the audience you want or need for your blog.

> **Smart Tip**
> One of the biggest expenses you'll have as a blog operator is promoting and marketing your blog in order to build and maintain your audience. This is a time-consuming process that will most likely cost money and require you to develop a high level of expertise in marketing and promotions. There are no shortcuts. You'll need to market and promote your blog heavily and on an ongoing basis by taking a multifaceted approach that perfectly targets your intended audience.

Planning Wrap-Up

Take as long as you need to effectively plan your blog. There's no better time to tinker and test your business idea than before you get started. After launch, you'll have committed your time and money to one path or another, so try to be sure when heading into the venture that it's the right one.

Review your objectives once everything is underway, and make sure you've built a solid plan for growth. If you know someone with blogging experience, consider having her or him review your plan and offer guidance as a mentor. Before actually getting started with your blog, make sure you've properly considered every aspect of the creative and business aspects of it. If you've done your job well, you'll have built a solid foundation from which your blog and business can and will grow.

Now that we've discussed the foundation required for starting a blog, let's learn more about what's required to actually create and publish a blog. That's the focus of Chapter 2.

2

Publishing Your Blog or Vlog

When it comes to publishing your blog or vlog content, there are literally hundreds of applications and online-based hosting services you can choose from. They range in price from free to charging a hosting fee of $10 to over $100 per month, depending on your needs. Some are well-known, owned and operated by huge online companies, like Google, while others are much smaller operations.

While not all of the available blogging services and publishing options are showcased within this chapter, what you'll find here is a comprehensive introduction and sampling of what's available. Between their content creation, layout and design tools, and their blog management tools, these publishing options can meet the initial needs of most bloggers and vloggers.

There are many books, websites, and even other blogs devoted to helping first-time users get set up with each of the popular services and applications, like Blogger, TypePad, WordPress, YouTube, and Twitter. Also, each service typically provides extensive instructions for getting started. Because each offers a different array of services, features, and functionality, your best bet is to carefully define your needs first (based on the goals for your blog or vlog), then contact each service's website or technical support department to learn about the latest feature offerings, and for instructions on how to begin using their respective service or application.

Consider Hiring a Freelancer to Help You Get Started

If you have no graphic design or website design experience, consider paying a freelancer between $100 and $300 to help you initially set up your blog and then customize a blog template for you. This also applies to branding and customizing a YouTube channel.

Working with a freelancer initially will help to ensure everything gets set up correctly and that you launch your blog (or YouTube channel) with a unique and personalized appearance (layout and design) that's based on your specific needs and that will appeal to your target audience.

No matter which blogging service you ultimately use, once the blog is set up and the template you choose has been customized, as the blogger, you can then create and publish new posts to the blog easily and from virtually anywhere that includes text, photos, and/or video using a computer, tablet, or smartphone.

While a freelancer with expertise in graphic design or website design can initially be used to help you get started, based on your skills as a writer, you might also consider hiring a freelance editor to edit your blog posts before they're published. This will ensure the content is free of spelling and grammatical errors and that it's easily readable using language that caters to your audience.

It's essential that your blog convey a sense of professionalism in order for you to build up credibility as a blogger and to build and/or maintain the reputation of the company the blog will be representing. Thus, the blog's layout and design should look professional, and the content should be well-written and free of errors. You also want to make sure that it conveys the right attitude and is properly branded.

Likewise, if you plan to incorporate illustrations, artwork, computer graphics, photography, or video into your blog, you can hire freelancers who can inexpensively create this content from scratch. This will help to ensure your blog's content is unique and that you don't accidentally violate anyone else's copyrights by using content that doesn't belong to you.

Hiring freelancers to help you in these endeavors can be done using an online service, like eLance (www.elance.com). You could also seek out local professionals in your community through referrals, or consider hiring local college interns who have developed a specific area of expertise that you currently lack as a blogger.

Community Blogging Services

As blogging continues to grow in popularity, many online social networking sites that originally didn't offer blogging services have begun to do so. For example, anyone can create a blog for free using a personal Facebook page or create a separate Facebook page for their company, group, or organization.

If you use a service like Facebook as your primary blogging platform, keep in mind your options for displaying ads in conjunction with your blog are limited to the opportunities Facebook offers. Your ability to directly sell themed merchandise or products through a Facebook page is also limited. Yet, Facebook does offer a robust set of tools for creating a personal or company Facebook page that allows you to maintain a blog and then utilize Facebook's free and fee-based tools for attracting followers to it.

Regardless of which service you use to host your blog, when it comes time to promoting it and building your audience, you'll definitely want to utilize Facebook, Twitter, and the other popular online social networking services.

Anyone can design, create, and publish a free blog using a service like Blogger.com very quickly. However, if the features offered by this or a similar service, combined with the widgets available for the blogging platform, aren't customizable or robust enough to meet your needs, consider using one of the more advanced blogging services, such as WordPress.com (which ultimately requires more of a learning curve from the blogger's standpoint, due to its more advanced and customizable features).

Web-Based Blogging Services

The following online-based blogging services are ideal for creating traditional text-based blogs that also incorporate photos, graphics, video, or audio content. Each of these services has its own set of online-based tools for creating, editing, publishing, and managing content.

Blogger.com

Blogger was launched in 1999 by Pyra Labs, a software company in San Francisco, and was one of the pioneers of the blogging movement. Some credit Blogger for popularizing the blog format, and even the term "blog."

In 2003, the service was purchased and made free to the public by Google, the Mountain View, California, search-engine juggernaut. Google has continued the development of Blogger. Today, Blogger.com seamlessly integrates with many of Google's other online services, making it easy to use, while providing bloggers with a diverse set of customizable tools, features, and templates.

Today, Blogger offers some of the most advanced blogging tools and functionality available at the best possible price—free! Anyone can create, publish, manage, and promote a blog using the Blogger service because it requires no programming knowledge to use, and has a vast library of options, widgets, and templates. Blogger also offers free tools for monetizing your blog by incorporating optional text-based and display ads within it.

Blogger is currently one of the most commonly used blogging services on the internet. First-time bloggers enjoy that Blogger is fast to set up, easy to use, and doesn't charge a cent for any of its services. All the blog creation, publishing, and management tools are point-and-click. Blogger also doesn't limit users in terms of traffic, storage space, or even the number of blogs you can create.

Because it's owned and operated by Google, it is one of the most stable and reliable blogging services on the web. One of the biggest benefits to using Blogger.com is that it seamlessly integrates with the Google search engine. Thus, you can set up the blog to automatically provide the information needed by Google to have each new post

> Tip...
>
> **Smart Tip**
>
> Like many of the blogging services, Blogger.com has its own proprietary iPhone and iPad app that allows bloggers to manage their blog, as well as create and post content to it, from virtually anywhere. The free Blogger.com app is available from the App Store.

quickly added to the world's most popular search engine. This makes it much easier for people to find and access your blog, and it helps to improve SEO results not just for your blog, but for your website or whatever other online presence that's associated with you or your business.

In addition, Google offers bloggers who use Blogger free access to detailed and real-time stats, thanks to Google Analytics. This helps you track and analyze blog traffic and learn a lot of valuable information about your blog's actual audience.

Another Blogger feature allows you to choose whether or not your audience will be able to publish comments related to each posting. If you do allow for comments, as the blogger, you're provided with optional tools for reviewing comments before they're published online and made viewable by the public. Allowing your audience to publish comments and interact with you, the blogger, as well as other people who read your blog, will assist you in transforming your blog into an interactive community. This dramatically enhances the quality of engagement people have when accessing your blog.

Tip...

Smart Tip

Once a blog is established using any service, there are a variety of tools available to help you promote it. For example, Weblogs.com notifies readers of all the latest posts to registered blogs across the internet. Often people find new blogs to read and follow by visiting here. There is a wide range of other services available to help bloggers promote their blogs, such as www.blogcatalog.com, Technorati (http://technorati.com/blogs/directory), and StumbleUpon.com.

For more advanced bloggers, Blogger allows you access to your blog's template code, which means you have the ability to display advertisements from private sponsors and other non-Google ad networks, plus add a wide range of specialized functionality to your blog.

When you register your blog with Wordpress.com or Blogger.com, for example, you'll automatically be assigned a URL. As a professional blogger, hosting your blog as a subdomain of any host isn't acceptable. You'll definitely want to register your own domain name and set it, within your chosen registrar's domain name manager, to redirect all traffic to your assigned URL address. If you'd like even more control over your blog, Blogger offers more advanced methods of publishing.

In addition to using the default (and free) setting of publishing your blog, Blogger allows bloggers to publish blogs on third-party web hosts (additional fees may apply). This is a method of publishing where bloggers use the Blogger service and tools to create their blog content, just as they normally would, but upon clicking "Publish," their blog posts are sent to a specified server. This option is easy to set up and provides the added advantages of more web server control. You'll need to register your own domain name and find a web host before you can begin using this optional functionality. It's useful if you or your company already hosts a website and you want to integrate a blog into that existing website.

Everything pertaining to your blog—creation, publishing, and management—is done using Blogger's web-based dashboard, the main control panel for your blog's administration. All your blogs and individual posts are listed on your main dashboard, with links to their individual management and posting pages. From your dashboard, you can configure, post to, or delete any blog in your account.

Clicking on an individual blog name presents you with the options of creating or editing posts; moderating visitor comments; viewing status; changing settings; changing the site's aesthetic template; adding AdSense ads; and more. Once you've created your first blog, click through the different options and features available to you.

If you're interested in giving Blogger a try, go to www.blogger.com, set up a free Google.com account (if you don't already have one), and simply click on the "New Blog" button. The site will walk you through the simple setup process, and you'll be able to publish your first blog entry in just minutes.

Google recently redesigned the entire Blogger service from the ground up, making it a more versatile blogging solution for individuals and businesses alike. The site offers extensive online help for getting started (at http://support.google.com/blogger/bin/answer.py?hl=en&answer=1623800), as well as video tutorials to help even non-tech-savvy people get started quickly, and then develop and maintain a blog that meets their needs and objectives, while catering to the blogger's unique audience.

TypePad

TypePad (www.typepad.com) was launched in 2003 by Six Apart Ltd., a San Francisco-based software company. The base program, Movable Type (which is covered later in this chapter), was originally written by Ben Trott to allow his wife, Mena (co-founder of Six Apart Ltd.), to easily produce her own blog.

The main blogging application was ultimately made available to the public for download and it enjoyed immediate success, which led to the development of the web-based version of the platform, in the form of TypePad. In 2004, Six Apart

Dollar Stretcher

TypePad offers a 14-day free trial. Sign up for and use the service firsthand before committing to it as your blogging platform. For more information, visit www.typepad.com/pricing.

Ltd. was able to purchase Danga Interactive, the parent company of rival blogging service LiveJournal, which was quickly integrated into Six Apart Ltd.'s offerings. The merged company now has millions of active users and continues to evolve as one of the most popular blogging tools on the web.

TypePad has become a very popular service even though, unlike Blogger, it's not free. It offers different levels of service with prices ranging from $8.95 to $29.95 per month. How much you pay determines how much online storage you require for your content, as well as the customizability of your template and the level of tech support you'll receive from the company.

> Tip...
>
> **Smart Tip**
>
> Customizable sidebars are a necessity for any professional blogger. The content you place here can be used to help generate revenue. A similar feature is available through WordPress.com and other blogging services. Typically, sidebars are used to provide ancillary content within a blog—not the actual blog posts. For example, many bloggers use sidebars to display ads, a list of recent post titles, and/or a search field.

Many professional bloggers prefer TypePad to Blogger, because it doesn't cater to the beginner crowd. The service focuses on offering powerful features, attractive and easy-to-navigate templates, extensive customization, and easy integration of revenue streams.

TypePad provides highly customizable sidebars, which is a benefit to any professional blogger. These sidebars, through modules that TypePad calls TypeLists, can be configured to hold advertisements, photo albums, Amazon.com book links, music, and anything else you can insert by pasting a snippet of code. This means that you're not stuck with one advertising network, blogroll template, or revenue stream. You have complete control of your sidebar content.

TypePad provides archiving of posts, the depth of which depends on your service subscription. It allows for the integration of podcasting and videos, scheduling posts, posting via email or mobile device, RSS feeds, and has some of the most attractive default templates available. TypePad goes out of its way to be a fully featured, web-based blogging service.

In addition to allowing outside advertising networks, TypePad offers its own revenue-producing services. For example, there are TipJar and TypePad text ads. The setup of these services is comparable to Blogger and Google AdSense ads—easy. You simply designate that you would like to take advantage of these features in your blog settings, and you're all set to begin earning money. TypePad also provides a tool to track your earnings over time.

TipJar is a simple donation feature that allows your blog readers to contribute financially to your blog. All donations are deposited into your TypePad earning

> **Beware!**
> Blogging services that provide their own advertising delivery systems may not allow bloggers to use outside ad networks. Check to be sure before signing on to a service. It may not matter to you at the beginning, but you'll want to know what your limitations are.

account, which can then be credited against your TypePad subscription fees or deposited into a PayPal account.

TypePad's text ads appear in the sidebar of your traditional blog, wherever you choose. These ads are automatically provided by TypePad, and change depending on the subject matter on the page on which they're displayed. They function and appear almost identically to Google's AdSense ads.

You, the blogger, get paid for each valid click on any of the ads displayed. The money earned per click depends on the ad that's being displayed; you'll have no way of knowing which ads pay what amount. All the money earned is deposited into your TypePad account and can be either credited toward your TypePad fees or deposited to a PayPal account.

If you're looking to accept donations, which is covered more extensively in Chapter 4, you can bypass TypePad's more expensive monthly service and set up an account with PayPal directly. PayPal will charge you per transaction, but there's no monthly fee, and the setup on your blog is quite simple. Likewise, if you're looking to set up text ads on your blog, you can sign up with Google's AdSense, and put them up directly on your blog as well. You can have more flexible equivalents to the TipJar and Text Ads service for a fraction more work and less expense per month.

TypePad is a well-respected and reliable service, and any professional blogger would do well to select it. In fact, TypePad offers a separate division, called TypePad Business Class (www.typepad.com/business), which caters to the needs of businesses looking to create and host a branded, professional, and feature-packed blog.

Using TypePad or TypePad Business Class, there are ways to give your blog a more professional appearance, such as the selection of your own domain name, customization of your template, and integration of third-party ad networks, but even at its default setup, TypePad produces a respectable-looking blog. TypePad also offers tools for integrating or linking an existing Facebook, Twitter, and/or Google+ account to a blog created and managed using TypePad.

> Tip...
> **Smart Tip**
> See firsthand all of the different looks and designs a TypePad hosted blog can take on. Visit the TypePad Showcase (www.typepad.com/showcase) to view actual blogs that utilize this service.

WordPress.com

WordPress.com is a free blogging service, like Blogger.com, that's tailored to casual and advanced bloggers needing easy-to-use features, yet a tremendous amount of customization. It's the web-based and slightly scaled down offspring of the downloadable WordPress blogging application, available at www.wordpress.org (covered later in this chapter). The success of the WordPress application spawned the web-based WordPress.com hosted blogging service.

If you already have a website or online presence that's hosted by an independent ISP (Internet Service Provider) or web hosting service, the WordPress application can be used to incorporate a WordPress blog to an existing website, for example. However, to create a standalone blog that's hosted by WordPress, utilize the WordPress.com service. Both offer advanced design and blog management tools.

WordPress.com users control their blogs through a web-browser dashboard that lets them write and edit posts and manage sidebars, templates, widgets, and all blog functionality. All the available features are easy to implement and configure.

While the WordPress.com service is free, you can purchase some premium options. For example, if you opt to host a free blog using WordPress.com, the service will automatically display ads within your blog, which WordPress receives revenue from. For $30 per year, you can get an ad-free version of the service.

If you have an existing blog elsewhere and want to transfer it to WordPress.com, for $129 per blog, you can purchase a guided transfer service. Meanwhile, each free blog account comes with 3GB of online storage space. To expand this storage space up to 10GB, 25GB, 50GB, 100GB, or 200GB, WordPress charges an additional annual fee, between $20 and $290.

An additional fee will also apply to utilize one of WordPress's Premium Themes. There are more than 50 to choose from, and each has a flat-fee price starting at $50. While a free account offers access to basic blog templates, Premium Themes have been designed to manage specific types of blogs related to online magazines, music, news, food, or photography, for example.

WordPress.com also offers a fee-based template customization service, which allows you to hire an expert who will help

Dollar Stretcher

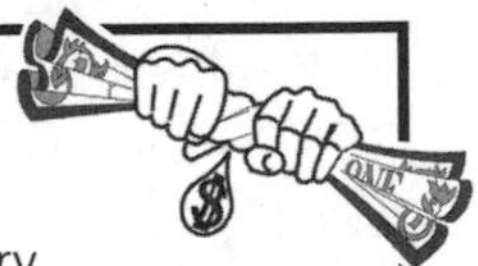

The various free blogging services vary greatly in quality and features available. Don't assume that all the free services offer the same features and functionality. Some are quite well-equipped, while others are very limited in terms of what's offered.

you fully customize a WordPress-compatible template to meet your specific needs or to help you properly brand a blog.

The main drawback to using WordPress.com instead of the installed server edition of WordPress is that bloggers cannot incorporate their own ads (via a third-party service such as AdSense) into the blog, and fewer widgets, plug-ins, and templates are available to customize the blog.

To check out WordPress.com for yourself, visit www.wordpress.com.

There Are Many More Options to Choose From

When it comes to choosing the ideal free or low-cost blog hosting service to meet your needs, pay careful attention to:

- The design, flexibility and customizability of the blog templates offered
- How easy the service is to use, and what type of learning curve will be needed, based on your existing knowledge and skills
- The reliability, stability, and reputation of the blogging service
- What tools are available to help you create, manage, and maintain the blog itself
- Whether or not a specialized app is available for your tablet or smartphone that allows you to manage your blog and create/publish posts remotely
- What integrated resources are available to help you properly promote your blog
- What types of tech support are available if you have questions or run into problems

Beyond the services you've read about so far, some of the other extremely popular and well-established blog hosting services that offer similar functionality to Blogger, TypePad, or WordPress, for example, include: LiveJournal (www.livejournal.com), Weebly (www.weebly.com), and Blogster (www.blogster.com).

If you're looking to host a vlog, YouTube is definitely the way to go. Start by creating your own free YouTube channel. However, you can also host vlogs using competing services, like Vimeo (www.vimeo.com) or Vine (http://vine.co).

There are also a wide range of options available if you want to create and produce a podcast. The best place to start learning about podcasting is from Apple (www.apple.com/itunes/podcasts/specs.html), which hosts the iTunes service and offers the most popular podcast directory and distribution service.

Once your podcast is established, you can also distribute it through other services, like Podcast.com (www.podcast.com), as well as your own website.

Installed Server Applications

As mentioned earlier, an installed server application is a blogging program that you must download and install on a web server. It should be used if you want to add blogging capabilities to an existing website, for example, that's being hosted in-house or by an independent ISP or web hosting service.

Each of the following applications comes with extensive instructions on how to install the application on a web server.

> **Dollar Stretcher**
>
> There are many quality, free, open-source blogging applications available for download and use. Don't assume that commercial applications are any better than the open-source alternative. Often that's not the case.

If you find yourself intimidated by the idea of installing and running your own blogging application, you might want to consider one of the turnkey, web-based services, like WordPress.com.

However, if you know how to wrestle an application onto a server, or if you're up for learning the task, an installed server application can provide you with more control and a greater ability to customize your blog than a hosted blogging service ever could. This section offers a brief overview of just a few of the popular blogging applications.

Movable Type

Movable Type is a proprietary blogging application developed by Six Apart Ltd., the company that also offers TypePad. Movable Type is a widely used blogging platform with many of the features you'd want as a professional blogger, such as archiving, trackback, and the ability to manage and publish visitor comments.

Movable Type also has a wide range of plug-ins available, allowing bloggers to easily add features and functionality to their blogs. This software is free to individual users but must be licensed to enable its multiple contributor and blog capabilities.

There are many published websites, books, reviews, and articles to help you become familiar with this blogging platform. If you find yourself lost while installing, configuring, or using Movable Type, a search on Google will quickly lead you to a solution. The Learning Movable Type website (www.learningmovabletype.com) is also a great place to start.

Due to the fact that Movable Type is so widely used, Six Apart Ltd. has been able to enlist the help of many web hosts and ISPs who will either install Movable Type for you on your hosting account, or will have it already installed when you sign up.

> **Dollar Stretcher**
>
> Finding a web hosting service that bundles a blogging application into its service is not hard to do and could save you some money.

Another advantage of Movable Type is the application's networking capabilities, which can come in handy when trying to spread the word about your new business. Movable Type introduced the concept of trackback to the blogosphere.

Trackback is a way for blogs to dynamically link to each other. If a blogger writes a new post commenting on or referring to an entry found at another blog, and both blogging tools support the trackback protocol, then the commenting blogger can notify the other blog with a "trackback ping." The receiving blog will usually display summaries of, and links to, all the commenting entries below the original entry. Trackback allows readers to easily follow conversations spanning several blogs. It's a great way to get a lot of links to your blog scattered around the blogosphere in a hurry. And it can bring in hordes of readers to your blog.

The interface of Movable Type is similar to TypePad's. It will list all your blogs for you on your main page. Clicking on your blog title will bring you to your blog management page, where you can perform all the tasks that you would expect, such as posting and editing entries, and managing your blog as a whole.

Movable Type allows bloggers access to their template code, which means that customizing your blog's appearance requires intimate familiarity with CSS and HTML. A feature as seemingly simple as inserting a list of links in one of your blog's sidebars requires opening the code for the blog template, searching for the specific code that creates the sidebar, and editing it as necessary.

Many such helpful plug-ins are available to cut down on the grueling nature of some of Movable Type's tasks. To see all of the plug-ins available for Movable Type, visit http://plugins.movabletype.org. Movable Type enthusiasts are contributing to the plug-in library every day, and with every contribution, Movable Type gets even better.

Overall, Movable Type can be a powerful blogging platform. The learning curve to achieve its maximum potential is steep, but ultimately can take you quite high. If you want to use an already-powerful platform that's far easier to use, and functions similarly to Movable Type, try TypePad. But if you feel ready to invest yourself in a platform and dedicate the next few months to exploring plug-ins, becoming familiar with bits of code, and researching help, then Movable Type will prove to be a powerful platform for you. Movable Type is available at www.movabletype.com.

LifeType

In existence since 2003, LifeType (http://lifetype.net) is an open-source blogging platform that's been a true pioneer in the blogosphere. It was designed from the ground up to allow multiple blogs with multiple contributors.

> **Smart Tip**
> The ability to use plug-ins means that new features are being added all the time, making the blogging application even more useful.

LifeType is free. Being an open-source project, it's free to download, use, redistribute, and even alter if you wish. You'll never run into licensing issues with LifeType, no matter what your intended use or number of installs or contributors.

It also boasts a sleek installation wizard, which simplifies the often brutal task of installing a complex database-driven application to a web server. Like Movable Type, it's extensible. This means that the user community surrounding the project has the ability to develop and donate plug-ins to make LifeType even more powerful.

Another nice feature is that LifeType is localizable. This means that the whole blog can be easily set up to run in another language. So if you have an international audience, and can blog in German, Spanish, Dutch, French, and so on, LifeType will work well for you.

LifeType also supports podcasting, mass file uploads, photo albums, blogging from a mobile device, and many other features that could be of interest to a professional blogger.

The downside of LifeType is that its administrative interface can be confusing. The menus and options aren't always intuitive, and you might find yourself searching for the tools you need until you really become acquainted with this application.

LifeType has many admirable qualities; however, if you're looking for a more user-friendly or customizable platform, try WordPress.com. But, as with Movable Type, if you're comfortable reading and editing code, LifeType likely won't pose any problems for you.

> **Beware!**
> Localization means that the labels on your blog applications' functions and features will be translated for readers of other languages, but not your content.

B2evolution

B2evolution (http://b2evolution.net) is a multi-contributor, multi-blog, open-source platform that supports language localization. It's free and, like LifeType, comes with an installation wizard for easy setup.

Like the other applications profiled in this book, a main page displays the user's blogs and configuration tabs. Clicking through the tabs allows the user to tinker with the usual configurations: categories, posts, template files. The sheer number of available tabs and subtabs in b2evolution speak to the application's many features but can be a bit overwhelming at first. It will take any user a considerable amount of time before feeling at home among the maze of tabs.

> Tip...
>
> **Smart Tip**
>
> Watching your blog's traffic closely will provide you with a good idea of your audience's reading habits, interests, and locations. You'll learn who's coming to see what, from where, and at what time. This information can also be used to measure the level of engagement your visitors have when accessing your blog.

B2evolution isn't necessarily set up with professional bloggers in mind. Placing custom content in sidebars involves editing template files, and customizing the look of your site requires some knowledge of CSS and HTML.

Like a few of the other applications, this latest version of b2evolution is extensible, so plug-ins are available to make some tasks easier, and more are being developed every day.

Like many of the blogging platforms, b2evolution also has robust anti-spam filters that you can customize to suit your needs. Comment spam is becoming a large problem across the blogosphere as spammers grow cleverer. Spambots are able to roam freely across the blogs, posting advertisements for nefarious sundries on every blog they pass. B2evolution allows you to automatically seek out and delete these advertisements as they're posted. It's the first blogging platform to so rigorously address this problem.

WordPress

Perhaps the most commonly used and flexible blogging platform available is the installed server version of WordPress (http://wordpress.org/download). This application is the precursor to the WordPress.com web service. If you already have an ISP or website hosting service, as well as a preexisting website, for example, this edition of WordPress will allow you to host an independent blog or incorporate your new blog into your existing website.

> **Beware!**
>
> Comment spam is a real problem and can make your blog an unattractive destination for your readers. It's important to regularly review comments posted to your blog before they're made viewable to the public.

WordPress is a free, open-source application, which means you have access to all the code and can customize the whole application top to bottom. It also means that WordPress, the company, doesn't have to (or get to) saddle the application with the protective restrictions they place on their hosted WordPress.com service. Another huge benefit to using WordPress is the vast selection of themes (templates), add-ons, and widgets available that allow you to create a truly customizable online presence. You can also freely display ads within a WordPress blog, but not on a blog hosted by WordPress.com.

> Tip...
>
> **Smart Tip**
>
> As you'll be spending much of your workday using your blogging application's user interface, it's important that you pick one that you find attractive and easy to use. It should also offer the features, commands, and functions you need to create, publish, and manage the blog you envision.

Where the WordPress.com service may fall short of what some bloggers require, the WordPress application meets and exceeds the needs of most professional bloggers. The WordPress platform thrives in an unrestricted environment. Not only have the developers chosen to allow access to the template code, making customization possible, but they've gone one step further than all the other applications and called out the code in the places that most often receive customization.

This makes customizing your blog's sidebars, headers, footers, comments, archives, posts, and everything else easier than in most other installed blogging applications. You'll still need to brave dealing directly with template code in places, but WordPress makes it significantly less daunting by pointing out what code to edit. Keep in mind, although there is a learning curve involved with mastering WordPress, you'll find a vast number of books, online tutorial videos (on YouTube, for example), independent webpages, blogs, magazines, and other resources that will help you learn the skills needed to get the most out of the WordPress blogging platform.

WordPress also allows you to create pages for your website. Their pages manager makes it easy to create static informational pages on any topic you choose. This functionality allows you to create an "About Me," "Contact Me," or "Merchandise" pages, for example. This is an extremely useful feature.

Several available plug-ins make integrating Google's AdSense into WordPress quick and painless. There are also plug-ins to help you integrate Amazon.com and other revenue streams. WordPress is one of the few installed applications that allow bloggers to integrate with several ad networks without touching a single line of code.

WordPress offers a vast number of aesthetic themes you can install for your blog and links to multiple websites that offer even more. Some of the themes (templates) are free, while others are fee-based. You won't have a hard time finding a theme to fit your needs, and if you can't find that perfect theme you had in mind, you have the ability to edit the code until you get exactly what you want.

The WordPress administrative interface works on the dashboard concept, just like the WordPress.com service. The interface is attractive and easy to navigate. Tools don't get lost in an endless sea of tabs. You should quickly feel at home clicking through the numerous configuration options.

In addition to all these advantages, WordPress offers all the standard features that you've come to expect from a blogging service, and because it is run from your own server or web host, you won't run into service limits and price increases. It is a high-powered blogging platform with great extensibility and an easy-to-use nature. Oh, and it's free.

YouTube: The Premier Online Service for Vloggers

If you decide to become a vlogger, you'll definitely want to use YouTube (www.youtube.com) and create your own YouTube channel. Recently, YouTube introduced the YouTube One Channel (www.youtube.com/onechannel), which makes it easy to brand your YouTube channel and make sure it's fully compatible across a wide range of computer and mobile device platforms. This is useful if you're creating and managing a vlog for a company.

When it comes to publishing video content on the web, YouTube is definitely the most popular service in the world, and it's free to use. In fact, YouTube's search feature is now the second most popular internet search engine in the world, next to Google.

Using YouTube, professional vloggers can generate revenue from their vlogs by creating a unique YouTube channel and by becoming a YouTube partner. The best source for learning about how you can fully use YouTube as a vlogger is the YouTube Creator Playbook, which is available for free online at www.youtube.com/yt/playbook/.

As a vlogger, you'll also want to explore the features and functionality offered by Google+ Hang Outs (www.google.com), Vimeo (www.vimeo.com), YouNow (www.younow.com), and the mobile video sharing service called Vine (https://itunes.apple.com/us/app/vine/id592447445).

Vloggers should definitely focus on creating a branded YouTube channel, but plan to promote their individual videos using a separate blog, website, Facebook page, and/or Twitter feed. Integrating YouTube videos into an existing online presence is a quick and proven way to improve a website's SEO, for example, which makes it easier for people to find your website and vlog using a search engine, such as Google.

Twitter: The Primary Tool for Microbloggers

While Facebook and other more robust online social networking services offer microblogging as a way for users to quickly update their status on their Facebook page and share one sentence worth of information in conjunction with a photo, website URL, and/or their location, the microblogging service that has taken the world by storm is Twitter (www.twitter.com).

Individuals, businesspeople, companies in all industries, entrepreneurs, celebrities, politicians, artists, charitable organizations, and countless others have all discovered innovative ways of using Twitter to quickly and inexpensively reach a vast audience.

Instead of a full-length blog entry, a microblog post (or "tweet" as they're called) can only be 140 characters in length at the most. A tweet can also include a photo attachment, website URL, and/or the tweeter's location. In addition to maintaining their own Twitter feeds, many bloggers use Twitter to promote themselves and their traditional blogs or vlogs, and many companies use Twitter as a powerful marketing and promotional tool.

People who use Twitter can access this service, or individual Twitter feeds, from any internet-connected computer, as well as from virtually any smartphone or tablet. In fact, one reason why Twitter has become so popular is because it's easy to maintain and monitor a Twitter account from virtually anywhere using a wireless mobile device.

There are countless Twitter apps available for the Apple iPhone and iPad (as well as Android and Windows Mobile devices), for example, that make Tweeting fast and easy from virtually anywhere. If you're an iPhone or iPad user, you'll discover that Twitter integration has been built into Apple's iOS (its mobile operating system).

Starting a Twitter feed takes under five minutes. Simply go to www.twitter.com, and set up a free account. Spend a few minutes customizing your Twitter profile page, and then start tweeting (the Twitter equivalent to blogging). If you're not yet sure blogging or vlogging is right for you, seriously consider tweeting first, and then working your way up. Tweeting is as fun and as addicting as blogging but far less time-consuming.

If you already have a website, blog, and/or Facebook page, use Twitter as a powerful promotional tool for driving traffic to your other online activities, as well as to promote your company along with its products or services. After building up a Twitter following, many companies use this service to announce online-only sales or promotions, as well as to share news and tidbits of information with their current and potential customers, clients, and/or fans.

There are many ways to build a Twitter following for yourself or your organization rather quickly. One proven method is to invest in the TweetAdder software (www.tweetadder.com) for the PC or Mac. This powerful and inexpensive software allows you to quickly find and reach out to potential followers using highly targeted keywords, and then manage one or more Twitter accounts.

We'll focus more on using Facebook and Twitter as promotional tools within Chapter 3. However, it's become extremely important for individuals or companies with an online presence to have a Twitter feed. As a blogger, it's equally important to incorporate a "Share" button to your blog posts, which allows your readers to quickly share your posts with others via Twitter and/or Facebook.

Within a blog, it's also very easy to integrate and display your real-time Twitter feed using a widget.

A Few More Thoughts About Blog Publishing

Well, there you have it—several of the most popular blogging platforms summed up in one convenient chapter. Because the offerings of these services and software packages are continuously evolving, it's well worth it for you to visit their websites, at the links provided, and read up on what's been recently added, fixed, or changed.

Later, in Chapter 6, you'll read a handful of interviews with well-established and successful bloggers who share their opinions about which blogging service or platform is the best.

As you make your own decision, be sure to carefully consider whether you would like the ease of use of a web-based blogging service (which is ideal for first-time bloggers), or the powerful customization of an application installed on a separate web server (which may be more suitable for businesses or bloggers with unique needs). Try out a few possibilities before you commit to just one.

Once you've chosen and registered for, or installed, a platform for your blog, and you know what type of blog you want to publish, the next step is to examine the various ways you can profit from your blogging activities. As you're about to discover, savvy bloggers have come up with many different approaches when it comes to generating a revenue stream from their blogging activities, and taking a multifaceted approach will help you generate the most money possible.

Keep in mind, if you're establishing a blog as a way to further grow or promote your existing business, for example, it probably does not make sense to showcase ads from other companies, potentially your competition, within your blog (which is how most professional bloggers earn an income).

Instead, as a business owner, you'll want to properly brand your blog with your own logo and messaging, and then use it as a sales, marketing, and promotional tool that will allow you to better communicate with your potential and existing customers and clients, and assist you in generating new business. Thus, the goal of your blog will not be to generate revenue directly.

It's important to understand that even if your goal is to become a professional blogger, this is not a get-rich-quick scheme. For most bloggers it takes many months or even several years for them to build up a large enough audience so that they can earn a respectable income using the revenue opportunities outlined in Chapter 4.

Almost without exception, the most successful blogs are created and maintained by people who have a true passion for whatever it is they're blogging about. These are the people who are willing to work hard for little or no money initially, but who focus on a long-term audience-building strategy that ultimately allows them to generate a part-time or even a full-time income from their endeavors.

Before you start thinking about how much money you can or will earn from your blog, you must first build and continuously grow your audience for the blog. Establishing and expanding your audience is one of the focuses of Chapter 3. Then, in Chapter 4, the focus is on the various ways you can make money over time from your blogging activities.

3

Promoting Your Blog and Building Your Audience

Blogging is a fun, often addictive, and extremely rewarding activity on many levels. The luckiest and most hard-working bloggers have discovered how to earn a living doing nothing but creating, producing, managing, and promoting their blog. Countless others have found ways to incorporate a blog into their personal or professional lives, and at the same time, generate a small, but steady stream of revenue from it. Meanwhile, some people use blogging as a powerful sales, marketing, public relations, or promotional tool for themselves, a company, a product, or a service.

It's no secret that everyone would like to get paid for doing what they love. If you have a passion for blogging, the secret you need to uncover is how to generate revenue from it so your blog transforms from a fun hobby into a lucrative business venture.

As you'll discover, blogging is a great way to earn some money while writing about the topic(s) you're truly passionate about. However, blogging is not a get-rich-quick scheme or a guaranteed moneymaker. If you do wind up earning a significant amount of revenue as a direct result of blogging, it will be because of your hard work, passion, dedication, and the significant time you invest into promoting your blog by taking a multifaceted approach to building an audience for it.

In other words, don't give up your day job just yet. Blogging can become a profitable venture for you, but out of all the bloggers in the blogosphere, only a handful have managed to truly become rich exclusively from blogging. Most bloggers find that their blog can offer a supplemental or steady second income, but only after it becomes established and builds a significant following. This could realistically take several months to one or more years.

The process for generating profits from a blog isn't always easy, but the first step is to build a massive and loyal audience/following. The best approach to achieve this isn't always clear, and the strategies needed to achieve this goal are different for everyone, depending on the type of blog (or vlog) they're creating, who the target audience is, what the goal of the blog is, and how well the blogger (that's you) manages to promote their blog. Building, maintaining, and constantly expanding your blog's following (audience) is an absolute requirement if you ultimately want to generate revenue from your blog.

Of course, if you chose a topic you're passionate about to be the main focus of your blog, the hard work you'll need to put in while building your blogging business won't always seem like work.

As we mentioned in the beginning of Chapter 1, you'll need to attain several things to have a profitable blog, including:

- *A steady stream of original, entertaining, informative, and unique content* that's updated on a regular basis, and that perfectly caters to your target audience.
- *Blog content that encourages a high level of engagement among your audience members.* In other words, they opt to post comments and/or share details about your blog with their online friends via Facebook, Twitter, Google+, or LinkedIn, for example.
- *A large and ever-growing audience that is interested in what you're blogging about.* How large your audience needs to be in order to earn a steady income from

your blog will depend on many factors, including how well what you're blogging about correlates to your audience's interests, how well the topic translates into something people will pay for, and the type of people your target audience is comprised of. In other words, some bloggers with a following of just 5,000 to 10,000 dedicated followers manage to generate a nice income from their blog, while for others, significant revenues can't be generated from the blog until their audience is in the hundreds of thousands or even millions.

- *Establishing at least one revenue source directly related to your blog.* Most bloggers take a multifaceted approach to generating blog revenue and simultaneously use several of the strategies described later in this book to both promote their blog and then generate an income from it.

By now, you know how to maintain a steady stream of content and the best way to plan your blog to attract a large audience. What you still need to be clear about is how to let that large audience know where to find your blog, and how to profit when it does. In this chapter, we'll focus on various ways to advertise and promote your blog to help build an audience. Then, within Chapter 4, you'll discover strategies for generating revenue from your blog, if this is one of your objectives.

How to Begin the Blog

So now that you've got your plan ready and your publishing system is all set up, it's finally time to begin blogging. Before you can go out and find legions of faithful readers, you'll need something for them to actually read, listen to, or watch. Building a blog from the ground up takes some time, and may be frustratingly slow for some, but there's no way around it—you must have posts (content) before you have profits—and creating the right content from the start, and on an ongoing basis, will require every ounce of creativity you can muster.

The First Post

When you first start blogging, those first few posts may seem pointless, since you don't yet have any readers. This is the perfect opportunity to begin experimenting and to set the tone and attitude of your blog and to tinker with design elements, for example. Now is the time to find your blogging voice.

In reality, your blog's first few posts are very important. Not only do these initial posts mark the beginning of your blogging career, they also announce to the blogosphere that there's a new voice in town.

Down the road, as your blog builds its audience, older, archived posts ultimately receive a considerable amount of traffic on popular blogs. Think of older posts on your blog as back issues of a magazine. At any time, your readers can click the mouse a few times and read or reread past blog posts with ease.

Thus, if you're creating compelling content, you'll discover that readers are often curious to discover what content was published on your blog before they started reading it, and they'll go back to explore earlier posts, or they'll discover your earlier posts as a result of a keyword search for a specific topic that's of immediate interest to them.

Tip...

Smart Tip

When planning what to write about within your first few posts, try to pick topics that are not timely. Try to cover topics that people will be able to read several months or even a few years from now and that will still be relevant.

Later, if you set your blog up properly, readers will be able to search for older posts using a search field and/or access a post archive that's been integrated into your blog. You can also sort blog entries by categories that you create, and then allow people to access old blog entries based on keywords or tags you've assigned to them. These functions can all be added to most blogs using widgets or plug-ins.

As you'll quickly discover, what you say in your blog is important, but equally important is how you say it and the approach you take to convey your content to your audience. That approach must fit perfectly with your target audience's wants, needs, and blog-reading habits. In other words, it's not just a matter of content.

In addition to what you say and how you say it, how you present your content to your audience is critical. For a text-based blog, this refers to how it looks on the screen and how visually appealing your blog pages are.

Color schemes, fonts, layout, and design elements are all important considerations. As a general rule, keep the design and appearance of your blog as simple as possible. Often, a white background with black text, and the utilization of plenty of white space, works the best, because it's easy to read on any size screen.

If you're a vlogger, how you look, the lighting, the sound quality, what's in your background, and what visuals your audience sees are all essential considerations. Production quality is important.

Think about what impression you want to give your readers and followers. Do you want to present yourself as authoritative (an expert in your field or on the blog's topic) or approachable? Do you want people to be entertained and laugh every time they visit your blog? Should they learn something, or have new information somehow revealed to them?

As you determine your approach, be careful that you don't come across as too preachy or pretentious. You don't want to turn away readers from the start, or give people the wrong impression about you, the blogger. Write a few sample posts before you actually publish your blog and make it available to the world. As you create each sample, use different approaches and/or writing styles. Then choose the one that you are most comfortable with. You style and writing approach should be natural to you.

Create an Identifiable Logo for Your Blog

Develop your blog into an identifiable brand. If you're starting a blog from scratch, consider having a unique logo designed for it, and begin to develop an entire brand and visual identity around the blog. Or, if you're developing a blog for your company, incorporate your existing logo, branding, and slogans, for example, to maintain continuity.

If you have no artistic skill whatsoever, for less than $100, you can hire a freelance graphic artist to design a logo for your blog, typically in less than a few days. You can find freelance graphic artists using a service like eLance.com, for example.

When the blog *Jason Rich's Featured App of the Week* (www.FeaturedAppOfTheWeek.com) was first being created, using eLance.com, a graphic designer was hired for $75 to create a full-color logo for the blog. After the artist was given a short description of the blog and what was needed, the logo was completed in less than 48 hours.

After initially posting a listing on eLance.com, more than 50 graphic artists bid for the project within two hours, and each provided their portfolio of sample work. After perusing through the portfolios and bids, hiring a graphic designer to develop the logo required a single mouse click, payment via PayPal, and a few paragraphs of text to further explain the goal of the blog, the type of logo that was desired, and information about how the logo would be used.

The logo you use for your blog should fit perfectly with the overall layout and design, as well as the color scheme of the blog, and the logo itself should appeal to your target audience. It should also somehow relate directly to the blog's content from a visual standpoint. Incorporating a logo into a blog also helps to add a greater sense of professionalism and credibility to the project.

Your first few posts should be used to introduce yourself, explain your reason(s) for starting the blog, and announce your blog's purpose and goals. A reader who is part of your target audience should immediately identify with what you have to say, right from the start. Otherwise, you'll need to fine-tune your approach.

Think about what your future readers will want to know. Include any credentials you may have on the topic, why you find the subject interesting, and what you hope to accomplish through blogging. Also, try to include some fun personal anecdotes, if appropriate.

> Tip...
>
> **Smart Tip**
>
> Any writing style that's forced will strike your readers as disingenuous. Be yourself in your blog. Or, if you're creating a persona, make sure that the blogging personality you're adopting is likeable and believable—based on who your audience will be comprised of.

Often readers like to know some personal details about the blogger. After reading a handful of posts, your audience should feel like they know you. Over time, you want your audience to think of you as their friend—someone they know very well, and who they can trust and can rely on.

Focus On Descriptive Titles and Filenames

One of the ways you can build an audience for your blog is to make it very easy to find on the popular search engines, such as Google and Yahoo!. The best and fastest way to do this is to understand that each search engine will analyze the text content within your blog and categorize it based on each post's title; keywords that appear in the text, blog, and post-related descriptions; photo captions; the tags you assign to each post; and other content that it can recognize.

Think carefully about the title of each blog entry, as well as the title of your overall blog. Within the first 50 characters, try to include as many descriptive keywords as possible that people might use within a search engine to find your blog.

Then, within your blog, utilize as many relevant and descriptive keywords as possible, without being overly repetitive. If you opt to include photos within your blog, make sure you create file names and captions for each digital image that are descriptive and relevant.

Finally, when generating a list of keywords or tags that are associated with each blog entry, come up with a list that is directly relevant to your overall blog, as well as to that specific blog entry. The listing and recurrence of keywords you create will help the search engines properly categorize your blog. Think about what keywords someone might enter into Google or Yahoo! in order to initially find your blog. Then, associate those keywords and phrases with your blog.

> **Smart Tip**
> When including photos within your blog posts, create descriptive file names for your images. Thus, when someone enters a relevant keyword into Google Images or Yahoo! Images, for example, your blog's images will show up as search results. With the right file name and caption, these images can lead people directly to your blog. So, instead of naming a digital image something generic, like IMG_123.jpg, choose something descriptive and relevant to your specific blog.

For example, if your blog is about the Apple iPhone and iPad and related apps (see www.FeaturedAppOfTheWeek.com), some of the keywords or tags you might associate with the blog and individual blog posts include the blogger's full name and the blog title, as well as words like: Apple, iPhone, iPad, iPad mini, iPhone5S, iPhone5C, iPhone 5, iPhone 4S, iPhone apps, iPad apps, new apps, productivity apps, entertainment apps, travel apps, news apps, app reviews, app ratings, tablet apps, and smartphone apps.

Use a keyword generation tool, like the one offered by Google (www.googlekeywordtool.com) to help you create a list of commonly used search words, tags, or phrases that are relevant to each post before you publish it.

The First Months of Blogging

The first four to eight weeks in your blog's life are important. In this time you'll learn a lot about your business, your blogging platform, and your audience. These will not be profitable weeks, but the content you create and the fine-tuning will quickly prove valuable. Again, this is a time to experiment, learn, and fine-tune, yet continue to provide a high level of content that perfectly targets your audience.

Filling Your Archive

Once your blogging is underway, you should get on a steady schedule of updating your blog with new posts. How often you do this is up to you, but plan on creating new content at least once per week if you want to keep your audience interested.

Some blogs are successful only if they're updated multiple times throughout each day, so you'll need to create a posting/publishing schedule based on your blog's topic, goals, and the audience's demand.

> **Smart Tip**
> Once you establish a publishing schedule for your blog, announce it to your audience, and then make sure you stick to it. If you read the Sunday edition of *The New York Times*, for example, how would you feel if it was delivered to your door on Tuesday, because the newspaper's publisher didn't feel like publishing the Sunday edition on Sunday?

Once you're comfortable with the content creation and publishing aspect of your blog, and it's running smoothly, you can start thinking about the revenue-generating opportunities available and get down to the business of your blogging business. You should build up a few weeks of posts in your archive first, so that when readers do visit your blog, it doesn't appear to be a fly-by-night operation.

> **Tip...**
>
> **Smart Tip**
>
> If you feel the need to vent about something off-topic, consider starting a separate blog to publish these posts, unless they're directly related to your blog's topic and what you have to say won't confuse readers or take away from the blog's credibility. If you do voice an opinion, as opposed to facts, make sure this is obvious with your writing style. Don't mix news stories and well-researched statistics with personal opinions, unless you're able to keep these things separate and clear for your reader.

Starting immediately, post to the blog with the regularity you expect to have once the blog is fully established. If you post too infrequently, because you spend too much time polishing your entries, your blog will appear to provide less than what you intend it to. Likewise, if you post too often, with the idea that you should provide all you can as early as you can, you not only will run out of content to post fairly quickly, but once you slow the frequency of your posts, the readers that you have managed to attract will be let down.

Instead of posting every idea you have when it strikes you, create a separate list of future post ideas. If they don't contain time-sensitive content, publish posts to the blog over time. So, for example, if you have 14 posts ready to go on Monday morning, don't post them all on Monday and Tuesday—leaving yourself nothing to post over the rest of the week. Spread out your content over time so that you have a consistent and predictable publishing schedule. Your readers will appreciate and come to expect the predictability.

Consistency

If you're considering seeking private sponsors for your site, these first weeks also set the tone of your blog in the minds of potential advertisers. If you run a blog about the best window cleaning solutions, but half your posts are about national politics because that's what has your attention this month, window cleaning companies will likely shy away from your blog because you're not blogging about the topic that sells their products. Likewise, if you're too negative about products the advertisers are selling, they probably won't want to advertise. Stick to your topic, and keep your future sponsors in mind. Your readers will appreciate the consistency, too.

Testing Your Platform

These first weeks provide you with a good opportunity to really test your blogging platform. You'll want to be sure that everything is in working order before you begin inviting thousands of people to come see what you've created and published.

Check that the archive is actually archiving, the friendly URLs are truly friendly and easily accessible, the images load quickly, your content is easy to read and it contains no typos or errors, that weblogs.com is notified, and that your posts appear in the format you intend. It's also essential that all links within your blog work correctly. Otherwise, this will frustrate your audience, and they won't return. Many blogging platforms automatically submit newly published blog content to Weblogs.com and other related services. For directions on how to do this manually, visit http://weblogs.com/api.html.

Invite your friends, with their different computers and web browsers, to poke around the blog and report to you what they find. How your blog appears using various web browsers, on a notebook or desktop computer, as well as a tablet or smartphone, will vary greatly. You'll notice that your blog's appearance will also be different, depending on the version of a particular browser someone is using to access your blog and what browser plug-ins they've installed.

Keep in mind, Apple iPhone and iPad users who use the Safari web browser app to surf the web using their mobile device cannot view any content created using Flash. So, if your audience will include Apple mobile device users (and there are many millions of them out there), it's important that your blog be compatible with these devices.

Your testing friends may not find any software problems, but they'll probably provide you with a useful end-user point of view and offer comments, such as, "I couldn't find the RSS feed link," or "How do I access the archive?" Make notes on what they experience and improve your blog's performance and layout where you can. Everything about your blog should be intuitive, easy to read, and easy to navigate, even for people who aren't experienced with the internet.

> **Beware!**
>
> While the blog publishing services like WordPress.com or Blogger.com take great efforts to ensure compatibility with all popular web browsers, if you're creating a blog from scratch (without using a template), it's your responsibility to ensure compatibility with all the popular browsers and browser plug-ins. If someone visits your blog and can't access the content, or the content doesn't look good on their screen due to compatibility issues, they'll leave and won't return.

Beware!

Building readership takes time. Don't expect the world to show up overnight. Hard work and patience, not to mention aggressive marketing and promotional efforts, will be important.

You also want to make it extremely easy for your audience to share details about your blog with their online friends. To do this, in conjunction with each blog entry, include a "Share" button (this can typically be done using a widget). Upon clicking the "Share" button, your reader can share a link to your blog or a specific post via email or with their Facebook, Twitter, Google+, or LinkedIn friends, for example, with a single click. As you'll discover, a "Share" button makes it easy to build a larger audience through virtual word-of-mouth advertising.

If you've chosen to use a web-based service, you likely won't find any programming bugs, but now that you have content up, you should approach your blog from the reader's point of view, and make sure you have it set up in an easily navigable, attractive, and readable fashion. Consider color schemes, font selections and sizes, page layouts, on-screen menu placements, and where ads will be displayed, for example.

Attracting Traffic to Your Blog

Attracting thousands of readers may seem like a daunting task, and it is. But it's a manageable one if you work hard, have realistic expectations, and you're persistent in your efforts.

There's good news, however, that will help you with this daunting task. One wonderful thing about the internet is it's highly automated. There are many services available to you (for free and for a fee) that will make the job of directing internet traffic to your blog much easier and less time-consuming than if you had to do everything manually.

Realistically, there are only a few ways that readers will ever find your blog—through

Tip...

Smart Tip

Just one example of real-world advertising and promotions for your blog involves displaying your blog's URL (website address) on your business cards, company letterhead, product packaging, as well as on physical signage and point-of-purchase materials, for example.

If your company is retail-based and uses custom-printed shopping bags when someone makes a purchase, display your blog's URL on those bags and on the sales receipts handed to your customers. The more often someone sees your blog URL displayed, the more apt they are to visit.

Get the Vote Out

One easy way to generate hype for your blog is to register its content with Reddit and Digg. Based on a voting system that involves web surfers from around the world, Reddit and Digg are two free services that showcase links to interesting and timely web content that people want to see.

If you publish articles, information, or content on the web, getting that content highly ranked on Reddit or Digg, even for a few hours, can result in thousands or even millions of new hits to your blog. The easiest way to get listed with these services is to initially nominate your own articles or content, and then include special Reddit or Digg icons as part of your content, so visitors can vote for it. Then, ask a handful of your family members and friends to immediately vote for your content on either or both services.

The more votes your content receives, the higher placement it earns on the Reddit or Digg listings, and the more traffic you'll generate. To learn more about these two services, visit www.reddit.com (and click on the "Submit a New Link" or "Submit A New Text Post" button) and www.digg.com. Both services are free of charge to content providers and web surfers because they're advertiser-supported.

search engines, blog directories, link exchanges, advertising, promotions, and word-of-mouth. Advertising, promotions, and word-of-mouth can and should be generated in cyberspace, but can also be done in the real world.

Without a doubt, you'll want to promote your blog using your existing website, Facebook page, Google+ account, Twitter feed, direct email, and/or through ongoing participation on other online social networking services.

Search Engines

The first order of business for promoting any site or blog is letting the search engines—like Yahoo!, Bing, and Google—know about it. Submitting your site to search engines simply alerts them to your presence. They'll add your blog address to their web crawler queue, and eventually you'll be paid a visit by their web crawler robot for site scanning and potential indexing.

Keep in mind, when most internet users are looking for specific content online, they use a search engine, such as Google, to find what they're looking for. Upon doing a search, chances are they'll receive dozens of potential website and/or blog recommendations as a result of their query. Yet the typical surfer will only visit the first one, two, or three sites listed, so being the tenth or fifteenth site listed, for example, is typically worthless.

Most top-level search engines will find your site eventually, but the advantage to submitting your link to them is that you give them a head start on finding you, which often shortens the process from potentially months to days or weeks for a listing. Keep in mind, many blogging platforms will now automatically get your latest post listed with the search engines within minutes or hours, but you need to optimize your blog, as well as each post, to be SEO friendly.

Listing your blog manually with the search engines can be tricky. Not only do you want to be listed with the major search engines, but you want to be one of the first listings web surfers see when they use specific keywords or search phrases that relate to your blog's content.

This means you'll need to handle what's called "search engine optimization" or "SEO." This is a science and art form unto itself, and doing it right by yourself will take skill, experience, and knowledge. Many first-time bloggers opt to hire SEO professionals to assist them in getting their blog listed as quickly as possible with the major search engines.

As a blogger, you need to become aware of what keywords or tags (which are directly relevant to your blog) will attract the attention of search engine web crawlers, and then get into the habit of using those words or phrases with your titles, descriptions, photo captions, content file names, and within the actual blog entries.

How the search engines work is always evolving, as is the way they rank their search results. There's no way to guarantee that your blog will be at the top of any search results, regardless of what SEO strategies you use. In fact, there's no way to guarantee your blog will be listed at all. Books, websites, and entire industries are devoted to the task of site SEO.

Keep in mind, the SEO industry is plagued with rip-off artists who take advantage of a site owners' lack of technical know-how. You can submit your link to search engines yourself, for free. But if you're looking to have a professional do it for you, along with other optimization services, be sure to collect references before signing any contracts or paying high fees.

There's a difference between paying to have your blog simply listed with the search engines and having someone perform SEO strategies to ensure you receive a top-level listing. Services that simply list your blog with the search engines will be inexpensive

> **Beware!**
> If you use an SEO service, read their references and resume before you make a payment. There are many SEO scams that pose as legitimate companies that target first-time bloggers and website operators. Visit this website to read Google's suggestions for hiring a reputable SEO service: http://support.google.com/webmasters/bin/answer.py?hl=en&answer=35291.

(under $50), while an experienced SEO service might charge $100 to several thousand dollars per month. Make sure that you pay for results and not promises.

There simply isn't room in this book to provide you with the all the knowledge and theory that goes into SEO. Google, for example, offers extensive online articles that explain SEO and how to utilize it to promote a website or blog. You'll find some of this information online at http://support.google.com/webmasters/bin/answer.py?hl=en&answer=35291.

Google also publishes the *Google Search Engine Optimization Starter Guide* in PDF form, which can be downloaded and read for free. To find the latest edition of this publication, access Google (www.google.com) and within the Search field, type "Google Search Engine Optimization Starter Guide."

The following are the basics and best things to do to increase your blog's chances of climbing the search engine results.

Tap the Power of Social Networking Sites

Depending on your target audience, becoming active on Facebook (www.facebook.com), Twitter (www.twitter.com), Google+ (https://plus.google.com), LinkedIn (www.linkedin.com), or one of the many other popular online social networking services is a great way to build an audience for your blog, grow your popularity, and reach out to your target audience.

These services allow you to post public bulletins, email members directly, and find others who share your interests. While very targeted and inexpensive paid advertising opportunities are available on many of these services, you can become active on them as a member and generate free publicity for yourself and your blog with ease. In addition to popular online social networking sites, find services, websites, or blogs that are similar—with a focus that relates to your target audience—and become active on those sites as well.

Submission Pages for Top Search Engines

- *Google*: www.google.com/webmasters/tools/submit-url
- *Bing*: www.bing.com/toolbox/submit-site-url

For help with SEO tasks beyond simply getting your site or blog listed with the search engines, just a small sampling of the fee-based SEO services available include:

- *Build Traffic:* http://buildtraffic.com/indexnew.shtml
- *Engine Seeker:* www.engineseeker.com
- *Traffic Blazer:* www.godaddy.com/search-engine/seo-services.aspx

Keyword Optimization

The concept of keywords or tags is crucial to understand. Many search engines rely heavily on the keyword concept for ranking. All the contextual advertising programs you'll use to promote your blog or generate revenue by displaying text-based ads depend heavily on the presence of relevant keywords or tags throughout your blog.

A keyword can be any textual word or phrase within your blog—words within images or that are incorporated into graphics (or animations) won't count. Search engine web crawlers and advertisement scripts collect all the words from within your blog and report them back to their respective services. The service, whether it's an advertising company or a search engine, then filters out all the words that are articles (the, an, a), quantifiers (all, few, many, etc.), and attributive adjectives (his, her, this, that, etc.). What's left are the nouns, pronouns, and meaningful adjectives that hopefully give an idea of what the scanned blog and its individual posts are all about.

In the case of your blog, you'll want to choose a handful of words that accurately describe the content of your blog. Avoid adjectives, such as "awesome," as these will do little for you. Select keywords or tags based on two factors: word popularity, or the frequency that the word appears in search engine searches; and the word's profitability. Word popularity will help you get into more search engine search results; word profitability will help you make more money from advertisers.

Keyword Popularity

There are many tools on the internet to help you determine a word's popularity among search engines. If it's not clear to you that one word would be more popular than another you've chosen, use these tools to help you decide which keywords or tags to use:

- *Google Keyword Tool*: https://adwords.google.com/o/KeywordTool
- *Telepro's Google Tool*: www.tele-pro.co.uk/scripts/google/popularity.asp
- *SubmitExpress's Tool:* www.submitexpress.com/keytracker.php
- *WordStream Keyword Generator*: www.wordstream.com/keyword-generator

Keyword Profitability

Determining a word's profitability potential is less concrete. Think about potential items available that might be associated with the word in question. Say you publish a blog that reviews music, and you're trying to decide between the popular keywords "MP3" and "iPod."

In this case, "iPod" wins for several reasons. First, MP3s are nothing more than a file format. Even though it's possible to purchase MP3 files, they rarely fetch more than one dollar, and therefore advertisers won't spend big money promoting the sale of MP3s alone. The iPod, however, fetches hundreds of dollars per sale and is flying off the shelves. The competition in the iPod market is fierce, and the item fetches a high price, so advertisers are willing to pay more per click to advertise their iPod stock online. This makes the word "iPod" more profitable for a blog operator than "MP3" because ads for "iPods" pay more per click than ads for "MP3" services. Pay-per-click is covered in more depth later in this chapter.

Of all the words you originally came up with to describe your blog, you'll want to always focus on just a handful of highly relevant keywords, based on their appropriateness, popularity, and profitability. These will be your site's main keywords. Now, splash them around your blog as much as you can. Always use the same group of keywords whenever possible, but don't overdo it because the services that scan your blog are likely to block your site if they determine you're "keyword bombing"—boosting your overall keyword ratio by placing them unnecessarily.

For example, you don't want to include a paragraph of text that reads, "keyword, keyword."

> Tip...
>
> **Smart Tip**
>
> Keyword profitability is one factor used by professional bloggers when choosing a subject on which to base their blogs.

Search Engine Advertising

As a blogger, you can utilize Search Engine Advertising in two ways. First, you can pay to run ads that promote your blog as a way to quickly build your audience. Second, you can display ads from other advertisers within your blog in order to generate revenue. The drawback to this, however, is that you cannot control what ads will appear within your blog, nor do you have any say over ad content. Thus, if you're blogging to represent or promote a business, product, or service, you could wind up displaying ads for your direct competition.

Using search engine advertising (also referred to as keyword advertising) as a fee-based way to promote your blog and build an audience is an almost immediate way to begin appearing on the internet search engines. Top search engines—Google, Yahoo!, and Bing, their respective content partners, as well as Facebook, for example—allow you to place an advertisement along the side, or across the top, of search results pages for related searches. This is an incredibly fast-acting, powerful, and cost-effective way to reach your target audience, because your advertisement will only be shown to people who are searching for your content.

These ad systems all work on the keyword principle. Once you've applied and are accepted to an advertising program, you simply write out a very brief, text-based advertisement for your blog using the online-based template provided. Then you place bids for appropriate keywords in an ongoing Vickrey-type auction.

You'll pay the search engine the amount of one bid increment above the second-highest bid every time anyone clicks on your advertisement. If you secure the highest bid, you win the right to have your ad displayed at the top of the paid advertisement bar (or on appropriate pages) shown for any searches that contain that keyword. This happens for a specified amount of time, or until you're bid off the page. If you have the second-highest bid, your ad is listed in spot number two and so on. Less than 10 ads are shown on any given results page, so top spaces are limited.

Search engine marketing (SEM) involves using a service—such as Google AdSense (www.google.com/adsense), Yahoo! Search Engine Marketing (http://advertising.yahoo.com), or Bing Ads (https://secure.bingads.microsoft.com)—to place well-targeted, extremely short, text ads on the various search engines (and partner sites) that appear when a user specifically enters a search phrase that matches a list of keywords you've pre-created that relate to your online content and ad. Again, similar ads can be purchased to appear on Facebook (www.facebook.com/advertising).

SEM is an extremely easy, inexpensive, and fast way to begin driving traffic to your blog. In fact, once you set up accounts with Google AdSense, Yahoo! Search Engine

Marketing, Bing Ads, Facebook Advertising, and create your ad(s) and set your ad budget, internet users will begin seeing your ad(s) within minutes.

> **Smart Tip**
>
> From an advertiser's perspective, one of the best things about SEM is that you only pay when someone clicks on your ad to reach your website, blog, or online presence. You don't pay per impression (when someone just sees your ad but ignores it). Thus, you're paying only for results.

You can launch an SEM campaign with as little as $50 (or spend as much as you'd like within any time frame), plus you have 100 percent control over your entire campaign in terms of when your ads are seen, who sees them, and how long the campaign runs. You can also modify an ad or campaign instantly to fine-tune your approach or message and increase its effectiveness. As a result, you can target your ads to a very specific or niche audience in hopes of attracting that audience to your blog.

The success of your SEM campaign depends on several factors, including your ability to properly target your audience. This is done by creating a pre-defined list of keywords and search phrases that are associated with your ad. Your ad will only be displayed when a user searches for an identical phrase or keyword while specifically looking for content that interests them. Thus, it becomes your responsibility to create and fine-tune your keyword list so it allows your ad to be seen by the right people. How much you actually pay per click when someone sees your ad will be based on a variety of factors, including the going rate for specific keywords (based on what other advertisers are willing to pay and the popularity of those words or phrases). Regardless of which advertising service you use, there's a complex formula used to determine per-click rates, which can be anywhere from one cent to several dollars per click.

Online tools are provided by the various SEM ad services to help you fine-tune your keyword list that's associated with your ad, and then determine how much each click will cost you based on ever-changing rates and demand (among other criteria). Each unique ad can typically have up to 50 different keywords or search phrases associated with it.

Another factor that will determine the success of your SEM campaign is the ad itself. A typical ad is very short and concise, just three lines of text. (In some cases, such as with Facebook advertising, a logo or graphic can also be included.) The first line is the title of your ad. It can usually be up to 40 characters long. It must be brief and attention getting.

The second line of your ad is the description. It can be up to 70 characters long. Use this space to convey your main ad message. The third and final line of your ad is the display URL. This is your website, blog, or online presence's main address on the web. The actual destination someone who clicks on your ad reaches, however, can be different. For example, if someone does a search for "red socks" and your ad selling socks appears, you can have the ad direct your potential customer directly to the page on your site that sells socks, as opposed to its homepage.

SEM has become one of the most powerful tools website operators and online business owners (as well as bloggers) have to quickly and cost-effectively drive targeted traffic to a site (or blog).

Developing a successful SEM campaign will take creativity and fine-tuning. It's essential that you create the right ad message and combine it with the perfect list of keywords and search phrases. It's common for someone looking to promote a website to use multiple campaigns simultaneously, and then carefully analyze which ads generate the best results for the least amount of money.

Using this type of advertising, your goal is to generate the greatest number of actual clicks (which result in someone visiting your blog), compared to the number of impressions your ad receives. At the same time, you want to keep your cost per click (CPC) as low as possible.

Creating and managing a SEM campaign that's effective will take practice, but experts are available (for a fee) to assist you with this if you don't have an online advertising background but need your campaign to generate excellent results quickly, with minimal experimentation involved. You can find SEM experts through online referrals offered

Stumble Upon Offers a Fee-Based Way to Promote a Blog

For a fixed rate of less than $0.10 per click, StumbleUpon.com's Paid Discovery is an online service that will drive highly targeted traffic to your blog when potential readers are specifically looking for information related to the topic you blog about. Unlike other fee-based services, the rate you pay per click is fixed and extremely affordable.

What's great about StumbleUpon.com's Paid Discovery service is that you can set your daily spending limit and target your potential audience. So, if you set that limit to $10 per day, you know you'll drive 100 new visitors to your blog daily.

To learn more about StumbleUpon.com's Paid Discovery service, which can start driving new traffic to your blog within a few hours, visit www.stumbleupon.com/pd.

by the Google, Yahoo!, Bing, or Facebook ad services, for example, or by using a service like eLance.com or Guru.com.

> **Tip...**
>
> **Smart Tip**
>
> When readers see ads for your blog in the real world, you gain a level of professionalism for which most blogs strive. Implement this strategy slowly to allow for careful monitoring. Sometimes, if advertisements are poorly worded, badly designed, or appear in the wrong place, for example, the results won't justify the expense.

In addition to your ads appearing in conjunction with actual search engines and web directories, each of the companies that offer these advertising services also have content partners, which potentially allow you to reach a much larger and highly targeted audience.

Before signing up and launching an ad campaign using Google AdSense, Yahoo! Search Engine Marketing, Bing Ads, or Facebook, visit each company's respective website and learn what unique services and tools are provided by each. Then decide which company or companies you'd like to advertise with, based on your unique needs, budget, and goals.

If you're new to using this type of advertising, start off small, with a low budget, and see how it goes before spending a fortune on a campaign that hasn't proved itself. Also, carefully monitor the response to your ads to see which ones work best. The online tools needed to do this are provided by each of the SEM ad companies.

Without a doubt, if you're looking to drive traffic to your blog or online presence, dedicating at least some of your ad budget and resources to SEM is an excellent strategy and one that will likely generate very quick results.

In addition to these internet advertising programs, once you grow large enough, you should consider real-world advertising. Placing advertisements in appropriate magazines, newspapers, and such can produce respectable results as well. Marketing for a blog shouldn't be limited to the internet.

Blog Aggregators

A blog or news aggregator is a tool that retrieves RSS, Atom, or XML feeds from news sources, blogs, and other publishing platforms, and pulls them all together in one place. Aggregators are being integrated with a lot of web browsers and apps for mobile devices. This allows these applications and aggregator websites to list published information from all across the internet in one place.

The use of aggregators that's most applicable to bloggers' needs is in the creation of online blog directories. Blog directories pull together billions of posts from millions of blogs and index, categorize, and place them in easily searchable databases. Many visitors to these directories are looking for interesting blogs to read, and if yours isn't among them, you're missing out.

When establishing your blog, be sure to enable the RSS, Atom, or XML feed feature on your blogging platform, and submit it to all the aggregators you can find. For no extra work per post, you can make sure your blog is included in the search results of these popular tools.

Technorati

Technorati is by far the largest blog aggregator on the web. Start submitting your blog to the directory here. This service uses a system called "Technorati Tags" to categorize the feeds it aggregates. It's not a proprietary system but one Technorati popularized.

Technorati Tags' goal is to have every blog and every blog post tagged with a category. If your blogging platform supports post categories, and notification of updates to Technorati, you can already take advantage of this system. If you're lacking one of these capabilities, Technorati has instructions on how to take part anyway.

> Tip...
>
> **Smart Tip**
>
> Blog aggregators can lead new readers to your blog, but don't rely solely on them for new traffic. Your posts will be listed among billions of other posts, so you'll have plenty of competition.

Visiting the Technorati Tags website (www.technorati.com/tags) will give you an idea of the intended goal and the power of this categorization system. When the millions of blogs on Technorati send their categorized post notifications to the Technorati Tag system, the most popular post categories increase in font size, denoting their growth in popularity.

Participating in the Technorati Tag system will help you become a more involved member of the blogosphere and will place a link to every post you write on the Technorati website, where it is searchable and previewed by the millions of Technorati users.

Get Your Blog Listed within Blog Directories

Just as Google, Yahoo!, and Bing are popular web search engines that can help you find websites or blogs related to specific topics, there are more specialized blog directories that do nothing but allow people to seek out blogs based on their topic and keyword searched.

The Search Engine Journal has published a list of the top 23 blog directories and how to get your blog listed with each of them. To access this information, visit www.searchenginejournal.com/20-essential-blog-directories-to-submit-your-blog-to/5998/.

Link Exchanges

The main goal of promoting your blog is to attract blog readers. Where can you look for the highest percentage of blog readers? Why, other blogs, of course! Swapping links with other blogs is a great way to cast out a large net across the blogosphere and pull in a lot of readers.

Blogger referrals have a high conversion rate because readers most often trust that if their favorite blogger says something is interesting, it is. The exchange can be done in three main places: blogrolls, trackback, and posted links.

Link exchanges are a less formal way to get your link or ad displayed on someone else's website or blog. Contact other website operators and bloggers to request a link exchange. In other words, you offer to display a link to their site (or blog) if they'll do the same for you.

Choose sites or blogs that reach your same target audience, but that aren't your direct competition. You'll often find bloggers are amenable to informal link exchanges because both parties benefit from new traffic to their respective sites. Many sites and blogs create a "Recommended Links" section specifically to showcase links to websites and blogs their visitors might be interested in.

Blogrolls

Blogrolls are simply a list of links to other relevant blogs that bloggers often display in their blog's sidebar. The criteria for being added to a blogroll is set by the blogroll's owner. Some bloggers create blogrolls based on geographic location and some on content similar to their blog. Sometimes bloggers will list their friends' blogs in their blogroll, or even just the blogs that they enjoy reading.

It will be worth your while to visit blogs that have content similar to yours, that are in—or about—your geographic location, or are even just the blogs created by your friends, and ask to be included in their blogrolls. Ask in private e-mail and never in the comment section of the other person's blog—and aim high. There's no harm is asking high-profile blogs to include you in their blogrolls. Being linked from a well-regarded, high-traffic blog will boost both your traffic and credibility. If your request is accepted, you'll be asked to reciprocate the link in your own blogroll. Be sure you comply.

For more information about how blogrolls work and how to participate in them, visit http://weblogs.about.com/od/partsofablog/qt/WhatIsaBlogroll.htm.

Word-of-Mouth

One of the easiest and cheapest ways to generate new hits to your site and build a bigger audience is to encourage your existing customers, clients, or visitors to tell their friends about your blog and what it offers. You can ask them to do this out of the goodness of their heart, or you can offer them some type of incentive.

> **Beware!**
> Starting your own word-of-mouth campaign via email is hard to do successfully without crossing the line into spamming. If word of mouth doesn't take off initially, don't force it with more emails.

The easier you make it for blog visitors to share content with their friends, the more apt they are to do it, so consider incorporating within your blog's posts a "Share" button that allows readers to share a link to your blog or a specific blog entry with their friends via email, Facebook, Google+, or Twitter, for example.

Most blogging platforms make it easy to add a "Share" button using a pre-created widget that you literally drag and drop or cut and paste into your blog.

To really get visitors to support you, however, make their experience on your blog as enjoyable and simple as possible. After all, the real key to starting a word-of-mouth-traffic-avalanche is to create unique and interesting, or extremely useful, blog content. Nobody bothers to forward boring links to one another.

Become a Guest Blogger on Other Blogs

One way to promote your own blog is to pinpoint a handful of already well-established and successful blogs that target the same audience, and offer to be a guest blogger for those blogs. In exchange for contributing articles or blog posts, you will get credit for your work that can include a link to your blog.

As you'll discover, bloggers are always looking for new content, yet few blogs have the budget to hire writers to provide that content. So, if you offer a blog free, high-quality, and relevant content, this will help you get yourself noticed, develop a following, and spread the word about your own blog.

Post Reviews on Bookselling Sites

Another way to tell large numbers of people about your blog is to find books that cover whatever topics your target audience is interested in, then write reviews of those books on websites, such as Amazon.com, BN.com, and Apple's iBookstore.

Within your review, share information about your blog and explain how it can be a useful resource for someone looking for additional information beyond what the book being reviewed has to offer. Writing book reviews not only gets you and your blog publicity, but it also serves to help readers decide which books about a specific topic to purchase. Some amateur book reviewers develop large followings based on their postings on Amazon.com, BN.com, and iBookstore. You can use this strategy with other online booksellers as well.

If you adopt this approach, be sure that you post useful and constructive reviews and position yourself as an authority or expert on the topic. Then, add a subtle reference to your blog.

Don't Forget to Use Public Relations

Traditional public relations efforts involve working directly with editors, reporters, journalists, producers, and hosts from newspapers, magazines, radio stations, TV shows, newsletters, and other media outlets to generate free publicity (media coverage) for a person, product, or service.

This might mean getting yourself interviewed as an expert in your field, having your product reviewed, or making yourself available as an expert source in conjunction with a news story. Many bloggers are often able to get booked as a guest on radio talk shows because they've become recognized and trusted experts on a specific topic.

Media outlets are always looking for new feature or human-interest stories, products to review, and people (experts) to interview or profile. The best way to contact editors, reporters, journalists, producers, and hosts is to create press releases about yourself, your blog, and/or your company and its products or services, then distribute these materials to media personnel that cover your topic or beat.

These same press releases and materials can also be distributed to websites or other bloggers, as well as online media outlets, which can also generate free publicity for you, your blog, and/or your products/services.

When writing your press release, make sure it adheres to a pre-defined and widely accepted format. You can learn how to do this by visiting Publicity Insider (www.publicityinsider.com/release.asp) or Press Release Writing (www.press-release-writing.com).

Once your press materials are created, send them only to working journalists, writers, reporters, editors, producers, or hosts who would be interested in what you're offering. If you have a cooking-related blog you're trying to promote, don't send your press release to a sports reporter at a newspaper.

For a fee, you can obtain targeted mailing lists for newspapers, magazines, TV and radio shows, and other media outlets. While you can easily create your own lists, companies like BurrellesLuce (http://www.burrellesluce.com/Media_Outreach), Cision Media Database (http://us.cision.com/media-database/media-database-overview.asp), Media Contacts (www.mediacontactspro.com), and MyMediaInfo (http://mymediainfo.com/trialregister.html) offer customizable media lists that are reliable and updated regularly.

PR Newswire (www.prnewswire.com) is a fee-based press release distribution service used by companies of all sizes looking to generate publicity. This service helps you target specific media outlets, reporters, or journalists, then helps you get your press materials into their hands in a timely manner.

To ensure your public relations efforts will achieve their objective, such as introducing a new blog to the public and then driving traffic to it, consider hiring a freelance public relations professional who knows how to write effective press releases and who has established media contacts that will generate free publicity for you. You can find freelance PR professionals on sites such as eLance (www.elance.com).

Don't Forget About Real-World Promotional Opportunities

Once you establish yourself as a respected expert on whatever topics you'll be blogging about, go out into your community and share your knowledge in person. Offer to teach workshops, seminars, or classes related to your area of expertise. Most cities have an established adult education program that's always looking for new instructors and/or classes.

While you may only get between five and 25 people attending each class, the true benefit to you as a blogger is having the description of your class and your bio published within the adult education program's course catalog, which probably gets read by hundreds of thousands of people.

You can also seek out public speaking opportunities through local organizations, charities, colleges, senior living centers, libraries, bookstores, coffee houses, or places of worship that offer personal enrichment classes or workshops.

Using public relations and by reaching out to radio stations, for example, you can also get yourself booked as a guest on talk radio shows, or even start your own internet radio program as another way to communicate with and expand your audience.

Get Started Now, But Keep It Going

Regardless of how you decide to promote your online presence in order to generate traffic to it, your efforts will need to be done on an ongoing basis. Be persistent, and don't give up after just a few days, weeks, or even months. Most bloggers admit that they spend the majority of their time promoting their sites in an attempt to generate traffic, as opposed to actually creating new content or managing the blog itself.

Generating thousands or millions of hits to any type of a website is going to take time and effort, plus some type of financial investment, so allocate your resources accordingly. If you learn nothing else from reading this, understand that persistence, creativity, and a true understanding of what your target audience wants and needs will be the keys to your success for generating blog traffic.

A lack of realistic expectations in terms of how quickly and inexpensively an abundance of traffic can be generated is the key reason why professional bloggers fail and ultimately stop blogging. No matter what methods you use to promote your online presence, be patient and allow your audience to grow slowly. Also, do whatever is necessary to transform your blog's visitors into repeat visitors by offering them the content they want or need, or that they perceive to be of value.

4

Generating Revenue Directly from Your Blog

You should now have two of the three necessary ingredients in place for building a successful blogging business: a steady stream of content and a good amount of traffic. The final ingredient is the integration of a revenue stream. That is, if generating revenue directly from your blog is a primary goal.

As we've discussed previously, for many companies that plan to implement a blog in conjunction with their existing website, Facebook page, Twitter feed, or other online activities, displaying ads from other companies (potentially your direct competition), for example, is not a good strategy and can be counterproductive. Instead, you might want to incorporate some type of ecommerce or shopping cart element to your blog in order to sell your own products or services directly, or simply redirect blog visitors to your company's website, when appropriate, to generate sales.

Beware!

Realistically, using a subscription or paid membership model rarely works, since people are not typically willing to pay for content they can generally find for free elsewhere on the web. Unless you have a truly dedicated following and content that people find unique and valuable, consider other revenue-generating methods.

Bloggers who are interested in earning money for their efforts have found many ways to do this using their blog or vlog. Your chosen method, or combination of methods, should be appropriate for your intentions and content. For example, knitting blogs may have a hard time selling hats and T-shirts, while a blog based around a personality, for example, can become very successful at it.

Don't limit your revenue solution to just the methods described within this book. You know your audience better than anyone else, and therefore know what they'll want and what they'll reject. Don't be afraid to experiment with new methods of earning money or combining established methods.

Blogging as a business is a relatively new concept, and therefore old business models may not always be the most effective ways to generate revenue. That said, here's a brief list of established revenue-generation methods that are currently working for professional bloggers.

- Selling merchandise with the blog's brand, logo, and content (books, hats, mugs, etc.)
- Selling other products or services directly from a blog
- Soliciting donations from readers
- Participating in affiliate programs that offer high commission pay-per-click or pay-per-sale opportunities
- Showcasing advertising from other companies within your blog. This can include banner ads, display ads, video ads, or text ads from Google AdSense, for example.
- Offering premium content on your blog using a subscription or paid membership model

Donations

As a general rule, soliciting donations from your readers doesn't typically work, unless you're operating some type of charity or offering information that your audience deems extremely valuable.

Often, asking (or begging) for donations casts an unprofessional light on your blog. If you're providing a valuable service, you should be able to find revenue streams without resorting to begging. Relying on the charity of others is never seen as appropriate for a professional business or professional blogger. If you're aiming to become a top-earning professional blogger or hoping to earn a respectable income from your blog, soliciting donations won't get you there.

Donations do, however, have their place. If you're averse to placing advertising on your blog due to moral, commercial, or even aesthetic objections, accepting donations can be a suitable alternative. You can avoid selling products for other people, subjecting your audience to ads, and it requires only a little button in one of your blog's sidebars.

One of the best ways to go about accepting donations from your readers is to use the National Public Radio (NPR) model of fundraising. Instead of constantly hounding your readers for cash, hold a fundraising drive for a week at a time, a few weeks per year, for example. Devote the rest of your time to providing a quality service that your readers will be proud to support. Take down the donation button when you're not running a fundraising drive, as it doesn't look professional. Instead, place a small text link at the bottom of your blog where people can make donations between fundraising drives, and then restore the more prominent button once it's time for another fundraiser.

Be sure to announce when your fundraising drive is taking place a week or two before it begins. In your announcement, inform your readers when and why it is taking place, and how much you hope to collect. Clearly state the benefits that your service provides, and that in lieu of placing advertisements, you depend on reader support. Place a page on your site describing the details of the fundraising drive, and how the money that's donated is spent. Use percentages if you're shy about posting actual dollar amounts. Include on this page hosting, blogging service, ISP, and contributor fees—including your own.

Beware!

If you do decide to accept donations, either exclusively or in conjunction with other revenue-earning methods, avoid constantly pestering your audience for money. This will grow tiresome for your followers, and will push your readers away, potentially to other blogs, where they don't have to fear panhandling.

> **Smart Tip**
> A meter in your sidebar showing how much has been collected and how much farther you have to go to meet your fundraising goal is a great motivator for your readers to contribute. It's part of human nature to want to see those little thermometers pop.

When the fundraising week begins, place a few posts reminding readers that you're holding your "Annual [insert month or season] Fund Drive" and that you would very much appreciate their generous support.

The old-fashioned method of receiving donations as a check or money order in the mail should be made available to readers who might be wary of conducting transactions online, but you should also sign up with an online financial service that makes it easy for readers to contribute with their credit or debit cards. There are many programs that allow you to do this—some are strictly set up for charitable fundraising, others are part of a larger financial service. The ones profiled here are quite popular and trusted by millions of website owners and bloggers to handle their income.

PayPal

PayPal, which is owned and operated by eBay, has become the gold standard for online payment services. Anybody with a free PayPal account can send money (from their PayPal account balance, linked credit cards, or linked bank accounts) to any person with an email address. Although receiving the money requires signing up with PayPal and either requesting a check or transferring the money into your personal bank account, your customers do not have to sign up to pay you via the service.

> **Dollar Stretcher**
> PayPal offers an easy way for bloggers to collect money from readers, or for people to quickly transfer funds, without the need for a credit card merchant account. The service is fast and reliable, but there are fees involved for the recipient of the funds. This is the least expensive and fastest way to set up a method for readers and followers to pay for anything offered by a blogger online.

PayPal has become very popular as a tool to pay for items purchased on eBay and ecommerce websites because the company has developed powerful yet simple online payment tools for small businesses and organizations that are easy to set up and implement, yet the fees are reasonable. PayPal also offers an easy way for bloggers and online business operators to accept and process credit card transactions without a traditional merchant account.

Once you register for a PayPal account, you'll be able to create, through its "Accept

Website Payments" wizard, a "Donate Now" button for your blog sidebar. The wizard produces code that you simply cut and paste into your sidebar template code.

> Tip...
>
> **Smart Tip**
>
> An alternative to PayPal is Google's Checkout service. To learn more, visit http://checkout.google.com.

Visitors to your blog will be able to click on PayPal's "Donate Now" button, insert their PayPal account information or credit/debit card information into PayPal's secure checkout, and submit their donation directly to your PayPal account. The money is almost instantly available to you. PayPal takes care of sending receipts, notifying you of the donation, and tracking payments you've received.

For this service you pay no monthly, setup, or terminal fees, like you would for a credit card merchant account. PayPal charges per-transaction fees. To see the current fees that PayPal charges, go to their main site at www.paypal.com, scroll to the bottom, and click the "Fees" link.

PayPal is a powerful system with many options for customization. For example, if you'd like to present your readers with some payment flexibility, you have the option to set up a button that accepts recurring payments, allowing your readers to spread out their donations over time. PayPal will automatically charge the user's card according to the schedule you set and dump the money into your account. For more information, visit www.paypal.com.

Click & Pledge

Click & Pledge is a service designed specifically with fundraisers in mind. It has been around since 2000, and has been making raising money online easier for charities, shelters, and organizations. It offers innovative tools, such as virtual food drives, interactive "Click-It" donation buttons for your site, and those red contribution thermometers that everybody loves so much.

Some of these tools can be taken advantage of by all bloggers. Some, unfortunately, like the contribution thermometer, require that you take advantage of its in-house website management service.

Click & Pledge is a company devoted to helping you raise money. Like PayPal, it doesn't charge recurring fees, only fees per transaction. Unlike PayPal, it doesn't charge one rate for all transactions, rather it charges a different set rate for each different credit card system. American Express is the most expensive at 8.75 percent, while MasterCard and Visa are 4.75 percent.

Because Click & Pledge is set up exclusively to facilitate fundraisers, it's able to offer advanced fundraising features. One such offering is the Empower program, wherein it

> **Beware!**
>
> Unless you're operating a fundraising blog or working in conjunction with some type of charity, don't expect people to simply donate money to you as a blogger simply because they like your content. Very few people will voluntarily donate money to a blogger.

advertises a product giveaway on your behalf, through your site. Contributors are entered into a drawing for the prize item (which you select and provide), and then at the end of the fundraiser, a winner is picked. Click & Pledge sends off the item, and you collect the donations. Also, like PayPal, Click & Pledge offers the setup of recurring payments, giving you and your readers more options.

Click & Pledge provides wonderful support via telephone, email, and live chat. If you ever have a question for the sales or support staff, visit their site, click the "Live Chat" button, and you'll have your answer in seconds. You'll find this feature extremely useful if you decide to take advantage of its services. Visit the website at www.clickandpledge.com.

Other Easy-to-Set-Up Merchant Account Options

Whether you want to accept donations through your blog, be able to sell items directly to your audience, or sell services through your blog, you will need some type of merchant account in order to accept and process credit card and debit card transactions. There are a handful of companies that make it very easy and inexpensive to set up a credit card merchant account.

Many of these options have no start-up costs or long-term contracts. You simply pay a flat fee per transaction. To learn more, visit the websites for these companies:

- *Square*: www.square.com
- *Intuit GoPayment*: www.intuit.com
- *WePay*: www.wepay.com
- *GoDaddy*: www.godaddy.com/ecommerce/merchant-services.aspx

Affiliate Programs

Once you have substantial traffic (thousands or more visitors per month), other companies will want to profit from it. This is the central idea directly behind affiliate programs, and, in a less direct way, advertising in general.

Affiliate programs function basically like any other form of text, video, or banner advertising, in that you're paid to place an advertisement for a service, product, or company on your blog. What's different about showcasing affiliate program-related ads on your blog is how you, as the blogger, get paid.

Some ads you place on your site are passive—you get paid just for displaying them. Some ads you place on your site require action—you get paid only when your visitors click on that ad. (These differences are covered in more detail later in this chapter.)

Affiliate program ads require not only that your visitors click an ad but also that a sale results from the click. When a click-through from the ad happens, and then a sale is made, you'll earn a pre-determined commission on that sale. Thus, for a "big ticket" item, you could earn a significant commission.

For this advertising method to work on your blog, you need significant traffic seeing the ads. The ads also have to be perfectly targeted to your blog's audience and appear in a way that's not overly intrusive, but easily noticeable by your blog's readers.

Many bloggers have discovered that participating in the right affiliate program(s) and showcasing just a few, highly targeted ads within their blog is the most profitable revenue-generating tool available to them. You do not want to wallpaper your blog with too many ads or your readers will simply ignore them. It's best to showcase just a few ads that are well placed and of direct interest to your readers.

If your blog discusses the latest bestselling mystery novels, and your recommendations pull some weight with your readers, devoting a sidebar of your blog to the recommended novel with an Amazon.com or BN.com Associates affiliate "Buy It Now" button may do very well for you. In this way, your blog would function as something of an Amazon outlet store. You would need a lot of visitors and a lot of sales for the percentage you earn per sale to add up, but if you can beef up those two factors, this is a viable option.

Selling books isn't your only option. There are thousands of affiliate programs offered by every size and type of online retailer. Even Amazon and BN.com, as you probably know, offers a huge range of items—some of which may be suitable for you to sell from your blog, and for all of which Amazon or BN.com will pay you a percentage of sales.

If you think that the quasi-store blog format will work for your subject matter, do a quick search on Amazon to see if they offer appropriate items. Then, for a comparison, do a larger search on the internet to find any affiliate programs from sellers of similar items. You may find a better percentage per sale, and more flexibility in how you present their items on your blog.

Beware!

Affiliate programs with unknown companies are rarely lucrative.

If you can't find an appropriate individual retailer with an affiliate program, you could sign up with an affiliate marketing service. These services function similarly to the textual advertising networks in that they're the intermediaries for online retailers and advertisement publishers. Companies like LinkShare (www.linkshare.com), ClickBank (www.clickbank.com), and Commission Junction (www.cj.com) have large directories of retailers of all kinds who offer affiliate sales. For a percentage of these sales, these intermediaries will help you get set up with ads from retailers.

Merchandising

If you have blog content, an image, or a logo that lends itself to being printed on mugs, T-shirts, and mouse pads, or other items, you should consider selling branded merchandise from your blog. Not only is it extremely fun to see your brand printed on all sorts of swag, but it will help you with promotions and can earn you some extra money.

There are several ways to go about creating and selling your own merchandise. The first, and most obvious, is to trek down to your local T-shirt shop with a copy of your logo, hand it over, wait a few days, and then take home several boxes of cotton and polyester goodies.

Displaying your new wares on your blog shouldn't be a problem. You just take a professional-quality photo, price it, and place it alongside a PayPal "Buy It Now" button, which you can create easily after signing up for a PayPal Business account. PayPal also offers instant shopping carts for easy integration into any website. It's a quick and easy way to get set up with full ecommerce functionality on your blog.

Depending on which service you use to create and manage your blog, a shopping cart widget may also be available. You can then set up an online store within your blog in order to sell merchandise.

If you don't want to depend solely on PayPal for your ecommerce needs, you could open an eBay Store, a Yahoo! Store, or you could install your own ecommerce application. To do the latter, you'll need to have access to your web server and install a separate shopping cart program alongside your blogging platform and then integrate it with a third-party payment processor and merchant account.

Tip...

Smart Tip

If you're interested in adding ecommerce functionality to your blog or launching an ecommerce business, be sure to read *Entrepreneur* magazine's *Click Starts: Design and Launch an Online e-Commerce Business in a Week* (Entrepreneur Press) and *The Unofficial Guide to Launching an Online Business* (Wiley), both of which are written by Jason R. Rich.

This can be unnecessarily complicated for merchandisers just starting out. If you would like to test the merchandising waters, we suggest opening an account at one of the store services mentioned above. This way, you can determine the profitability of merchandising without too much hassle.

The quickest (but not necessarily most profitable) route to selling branded merchandise is to sign up with an on-demand branding service. An on-demand branding service is an online store that sells a variety of items that are basically blank canvases for your logo, brand, or funny quip. The various services available offer different items, such as mouse pads, T-shirts, bumper stickers, clocks, aprons, baby jumpers, and so on. Each item you select to sell will be displayed, with your graphics on it, on the customized and branded web page that the service provides you so it looks like it's your site selling your own merchandise. Through this page, your readers can purchase items, which are then printed and shipped. You don't need to worry about doing anything except setting up the store and collecting the revenues. The service handles the rest.

The disadvantage of these services is that they keep a hefty percentage of the sale price. You'll end up making only a few dollars per item, which, if you're selling hundreds of items, isn't a bad way to pad your income while filling the world with what are essentially promotional materials. Besides, if they're saving you time by buying, branding, selling and shipping the goods, they may be worth the cost—at least initially.

Ultimately, you can make a lot more money purchasing customized, branded, or logoed merchandise in large quantities, then reselling them on your own through your ecommerce website or an ecommerce component within your blog, but this option will cost significantly more money upfront.

When searching for a company to create and help you sell your "merch," visit each service and read through their pricing policies—each one works a little differently. Also, the products that are available on each of these services vary greatly. Be sure that before you sign up, you'll be able to sell the particular item you have in mind, and that what your customers will ultimately receive is good quality and not total junk. Popular on-demand branding services include:

- *Branders:* www.branders.com
- *CafePress:* www.cafepress.com
- *Direct Lines*: www.districtlines.com
- *Zazzle:* www.zazzle.com

Tip...

Smart Tip

eBay is a great place to sell items. They make selling online relatively painless. An eBay Store is a good way to offer products for your blog to millions of people real fast. Selling on eBay is also a great way to reach its millions of users for potential new readers.

Memberships or Subscriptions

Internet users have become accustomed to obtaining information and content online for free. Thus, getting them to pay for the content offered from your blog could pose a challenge, but it's not impossible. For certain types of exclusive or very specific information that's not available elsewhere, people will pay a premium via a membership or subscription fee. For this to work, your readers, members, or subscribers must deem all your content valuable.

At this point, moving to a full-membership business model as a new blog is probably not your best strategy. In other words, don't block off all your content from the non-paying public. It will only serve to alienate potential readers and create another barrier between your blog and your profits.

While a full-membership model will hinder your blog's growth from the start, there are some variations on the model that are worth considering. Selling memberships that offer other types of premiums can be quite attractive to your reader—not to mention that the "member" concept creates an aura of exclusivity surrounding your blog.

These membership methods don't need to be exclusive of one another. Many bloggers offer both ad-free versions of their blogs and early editions of their posts to paying members. Fiddle with these methods, and find the most profitable combination. Just don't fiddle so much that you annoy your readership. And don't be afraid to ask them directly if they'd be willing to pay for an ad-free version, early posts, or exclusive content. The more research you do, the better your experiment will fare.

Partial Access

Instead of restricting nonmembers from an entire blog, some bloggers are having luck with selling memberships to exclusive or premium content, such as different categories of posts, search functions, or access to a blog's archives.

By keeping most of the content free for the public, but requiring membership for exclusive content, some bloggers are able to maintain unrestricted growth in traffic, while offering incentives to paying members. Plus, by creating an exclusive section, and

Beware!

Keep in mind that unless you can find a plug-in or widget that provides membership/subscription and/or partial access functionality for visitors, or your blogging service provides them, it will be necessary for you to do a little programming to implement them.

awarding some of your readers with the flattering title of "member," you create an artificial desire to belong to your readership.

If you provide quality content and valuable incentives for membership at a reasonable price, this method could work well for you.

Early Edition

Another strategy some bloggers are testing is the concept of "early editions" of blog posts. Using this business model, paying members are able to log into the blog and read your posts several hours (or days) before they're made available to the general readership. This method not only allows blog members to read posts before everyone else but also to submit comments first and participate in discussions earlier.

If your content is proprietary, very timely, and contains up-to-the-minute news, information, or statistics, for example, this concept could prove lucrative. For example, if your blog covers a specific industry and you publish exclusive help wanted or job opening listings, offering this timely content to paid members in advance could be very useful for your readers—and profitable for you.

Beware!

With a blog, incorporating early edition access requires programming, a plug-in, a widget, or built-in functionality to be viable. Manually posting content twice in two different parts of your blog isn't sustainable. Blogging services, such as the installed server edition of WordPress, offer this functionality and have widgets available to fully customize it.

Ad-Free Version

If you're offering top-notch content, perhaps the most successful membership strategy is to sell an advertisement-free version of your blog. This strategy can be successful because it isn't based on exclusion and holding content ransom, which can annoy some readers. Your blog remains the same for the public but is improved for the ad-averse crowd.

Readers who don't mind seeing advertisements aren't affected by this membership method at all. And because they're happy to put up with your ads, you earn revenue from the general public and your paying members.

Beware!

The ad-free method requires some extra setup and potential programming (unless a widget that offers this functionality is available for your blogging platform). Ask your service provider the best way to go about setting this up for your particular situation.

Selling Display Ad Space

The standard and most reliable way to earn profits from your blog is by selling advertising space. Advertisers will pay good money to place their ads on your site if the conditions are right. In other words, if you can serve up tens of thousands or millions of targeted customers, advertisers will want to reach those followers by paying to run their ads on your blog.

In order to be desirable to advertisers, your blog must have reliable traffic and content that's relevant to the advertiser's product or service. Most text-ad networks take care of the latter for you by scanning your site text for keywords and displaying relevant ads, as we explained earlier. But signing up with contextual ad networks is not all there is to blog advertising.

When getting a blog started, signing up with Google's AdSense (or a similar service from Yahoo! or Bing) just to get some money flowing is a good idea. But once you're established, if you're looking to make even better money with your blog, you'll need to go a few steps farther.

As a blogger, you have several options when it comes to selling advertising space. Consider how you can make best use of the following advertising options.

Ad Networks

The invention of the automated advertising network was a boon to the online advertising industry. It not only simplified the process for advertisers seeking exposure, but it made the process a lot less painful for website publishers. No longer was the lengthy and arduous task of seeking out private sponsors the only option for advertising income. Now, with a few simple lines of code, every website or blog on the internet can display ads that rotate automatically, update as necessary, and are always directly relevant to the published content.

Advertising networks have been on the internet since the beginning. But the breakthrough of relevant textual advertising created a spike in the number of ad networks available to bloggers and website publishers. You'll have plenty of options when seeking a network to join. They all function similarly in terms of how they publish advertisements on your blog. But they all have different methods for how, when, and how much they pay.

CPC vs. CPM

Before you begin researching ad networks, you should be familiar with the difference between cost-per-click (CPC) advertising and cost-per-thousand (CPM) advertising. The only thing that's similar about the two pricing methods is their acronyms start with "CP."

CPC advertising networks pay you a small amount of money every time a visitor to your site clicks on one of the advertisements you display for them. This amount of money will be unknown to you as it is worked out between the advertiser and the ad network and is different for each ad shown. You, obviously, will ultimately learn what you earned per click in your daily reporting statistics, but it will not be available to you beforehand because the ads are served on your site in real time. The only way to increase your per-click revenue is through keyword optimization.

The largest complaint about CPC programs is that often the conversion rate, on which you depend for revenue, hinges on factors beyond your control. If an advertisement contains errors, is unattractive, or is simply written in a noncompelling manner, your revenue will suffer. Likewise, if the ad is not directly relevant or of interest to your readers, it will be ignored—not clicked on.

The other method that ad networks use, CPM, isn't based on conversion rates at all. In fact, no conversion is necessary for you to profit. This method is a more traditional approach to advertising revenue models in that advertisers pay website publishers and

Use Traffic Monitoring Tools to Discover Who's Visiting Your Blog

Before you can begin to project how much money you could earn from displaying ads within your blog, you need to understand your blog's audience and popularity. Most blogging services offer some type of traffic monitoring tools, either built in or that can be added as a plug-in or widget. Take advantage of this information. Study it and get to know everything you can about the traffic to your blog.

If your blogging platform doesn't offer the traffic monitoring details you need, you can sign up for the free Google Analytics (www.google.com/analytics) service, even if your blog isn't hosted by Google's Blogger.com.

You'll also discover many "premium" (for-a-fee) services that offer similar blog and website traffic monitoring and analytical tools. However, once you sign up for a service such as Google AdSense to display ads on your blog, traffic monitoring tools are automatically provided as part of the service.

> **Beware!**
> CPM campaigns are not suited to blogs when just starting out. You'll need to establish many thousands of visitors per day before this is a lucrative option.

bloggers some amount of money for every 1,000 ads displayed on their blog or page—whether those ads receive clicks or not. This can be a more reliable and predictable approach to collecting ad revenue because it isn't based on factors beyond your control. It's simply based on your blog's traffic.

The overwhelming majority of ad networks use one of these two methods, and both have their advantages. But the advantages of each can't be universally applied to all blogs.

Optimizing Layout

If you're looking to earn a living from blogging, you'll need to become familiar with the science behind visitor behavior and the psychology behind advertisement effectiveness and how it relates to online content. This will require some experimenting and data analysis. It sounds complicated, but in essence it's just the repeated process of tweaking some things and taking notes.

Success with any ad network is based on many factors. The amount you earn largely depends on your willingness to experiment with these factors, as they directly affect your monthly conversion rate. Simply plopping ads on your site won't be enough to maximize your generated revenue. You've got to tweak and test several factors, including keywords used in your posts or on your pages; placement of advertisements on your pages, and the color, size, and layout of ads—if your ad network allows you to change them.

When tweaking, change one aspect of your advertising setup each week, whether it's ad color, placement, or keywords. Track your earnings for that week, and make adjustments accordingly. You may find that blue ads sell better than the red ones, and that ads on the left sidebar sell better than the ones across the top of the page. So placing blue ads on the left sidebar will earn you the most revenue for those two factors. Once you've tested every factor you can think of, you'll have the information necessary to put together the most effective ad layout for your blog.

Unfortunately, your "most effective layout" will inevitably lose effectiveness as your blog's readers get used to your layout and are able to visually gloss over those sections they know to contain ads. At this point you'll have to test and reformat again. Once you go through this process three times, you'll have the layouts for three

> Tip...
> **Smart Tip**
> The most profitable blogs change their ad layouts several times a month to combat reader "visual tune-out" and "ad-banner blindness."

highly effective advertising layouts on your blog. When you find your conversion rate dropping again, revert to the first highly effective layout that you used and cycle through your readymade layouts when necessary.

Profiles of Ad Networks

Many popular ad networks are available to you. This section profiles a few that work well for bloggers. It's important to be happy with the ad network you join. It can make your business easy or miserable, depending on how it performs for you.

Each network offers different features. Some may have what you're looking for; some may not. It's important to find the one that best fits your needs.

Google AdSense

Google's AdSense is by far the largest and most well-known advertising network. When it first launched, it was just a tool to help advertisers place ads alongside Google's own search results, but it has since been expanded to help advertisers place their ads on many well-established online services and websites, plus tens of thousands of individual websites that are part of Google's AdWords program. It has the most reach of any network of its kind, and therefore it has the most participating advertisers—which translates into more chances for finding relevant ad content for your blog.

To say that the Google AdSense and related AdWords programs work similarly to the others would be true, but it wouldn't give Google proper credit as the pioneer and standard in this industry. Most ad networks are patterned after the example AdSense and AdWords set, not the other way around.

Registration for AdSense isn't difficult, but it requires that you provide your home address, contact, and tax information. Google will walk you through the whole process, and provide you information about off-site links where you can get the tax form you'll need to submit to them. AdSense pays advertisement publishers every month via electronic funds transfer or a check mailed to the address you submitted during application.

After your account is set up, you'll choose the sort of ads you would like to display on your site. You can choose between text ads or image ads, CPC ads, or CPM ads. Both text and image ads can be paid on either a CPC or CPM basis. One restriction to keep in mind is that if you choose to display CPM ads, your site will need to be approved—based on your content—by the individual advertisers of each ad. This can severely decrease the number and rotation of ads that show on your site, but image ads

Beware!

Some blog services don't allow Google AdSense to be used because they offer their own alternative ad service.

may attract more clicks as they command more attention, which may be a good or bad thing to your readers.

Once you've selected your ad configuration, AdWords will provide you with a snippet of customized JavaScript code for you to include somewhere in your blog template code. Wherever you place this code, AdWords will display your new ads—you'll begin earning right away.

Once your account has earned at least $50, AdWords will mail a PIN code to the address you've used to register with the program. Upon receipt, you enter the PIN code only once to verify your mailing address is actually the one to which you have access. When your account earns at least $100, you're eligible to receive a check for the full amount in your account when next time they mail out payment checks or initiate funds transfers. Funds are disbursed approximately two weeks after the end of the month in which your account topped $100.

AdSense reporting tools go above and beyond when it comes to providing you with useful information. On your main AdSense account page, you'll see an overview of the day's earnings, page impressions, clicks, click-through rate, and clicks-per-thousand ads served. Moving into the "Advanced Reports" section gives you a chance to see more in-depth information about the performance of your ads. The "Payment History" page shows you every click clicked and penny pinched.

Since every advertisement that AdSense serves is highly targeted to specific keywords, it's entirely possible that the ads served on your site could come from your competitors.

In the event that AdSense can't find a relevant ad to display on your blog, they have a cache of public service announcements (PSAs) from which they pull. When AdSense displays a PSA, you receive no payment when a visitor clicks on it. While it may contribute to the common good to display PSAs on your blog, it won't do much for your profits. If you find that your site is loading an inordinate number of PSAs, fiddle with the keywords you use in your posts and on your pages. Try to use more specific terms that people are more likely to search for online.

After reworking your keywords, you'll still see the occasional PSA loaded on your site. To allow you to make the most of the space on your blog, AdSense allows you to provide them with alternate content to load instead of PSAs. This content can be images, text, or even other paying advertisements for your private sponsors. If requested, AdSense will load this alternate content every time it can't find a relevant ad to load.

For more information about AdSense, Google provides a tour at their website: www.google.com/adsense. It's a great program for beginners because it is quick to set up, free to join, and doesn't require minimum site traffic levels.

CrispAds

CrispAds is a blog-specific CPC advertising network. On the surface, it functions similarly to AdSense: You register as a publisher, and after installing a snippet of code, you'll display rotating text or graphic ads on your blog.

CrispAds offers several ways to find advertisers for your site. The first is by signing up to display rotating, keyword-targeted text ads. These ads, unlike with most text ad networks, aren't determined by an automated keyword crawler that scans your blog for content. Instead, CrispAds asks you to select the keywords you'd like to describe your blog, and ads that target to those keywords will be shown. This can help or hurt you, depending on your point of view.

On the one hand, selecting keywords to define your blog topic will keep your advertising focused on the general content of your site, no matter what words the current post or discussion contains. On the other hand, these ads won't always be relevant to the topic being discussed on the page. They could help or hurt you, depending on the specific topic of conversation.

Another aspect to CrispAds that makes it different than most other ad networks is that they pay a standard $.20 per click on text ads. For most ad networks, this price is variable and dependent on the price the advertiser is willing to pay per click. Usually the ad network takes a set percentage and passes the rest along to you. CrispAds reverses that model and pays you a set amount, then takes what's left over. This, again, could be a good or bad thing.

Monthly revenue forecasting is made much easier if you know the amount you earn for each click you produce. You would simply need to multiply your forecasted traffic by your average conversion rate by the $.20. Knowing about what you plan to earn in the following months will help you budget accordingly.

The second method CrispAds offers is monthly sponsorship. If you choose, you can submit your blog to their catalog, which will then be shopped around to their various advertisers. If selected by an advertiser, your blog will display ads from

Dollar Stretcher

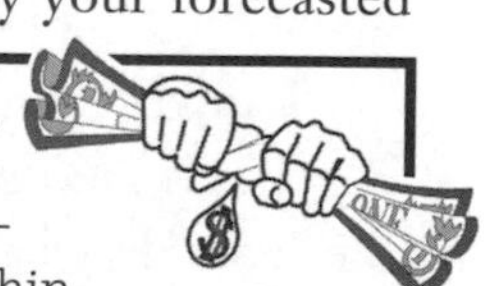

Displaying text, banner, or video ads within your blog can be a great way to generate extra income, but you don't always get to choose which ads will appear or who the advertisers will be if you use some of the services mentioned here.

that one advertiser for a month. The pay for this sponsorship varies.

> **Smart Tip**
>
> Tip...
>
> If you're being paid per click for ads you display within your blog, make sure they're relevant to your audience. Ads that are relevant and offer some type of deal or money-saving offer will improve your chances that your blog's readers will click on the ads, thus helping you generate revenue.

The third method available is to display rotating image ads based on the same keyword system that they employ for their text ads. Instead of a set $.20 pay-out, these ads pay 70 percent of the total revenue they generate. If the advertiser is willing to pay CrispAds $1 per click, you take $.70. Because they host fewer image ads than text ads, it's possible that, once in a while, CrispAds will not be able to deliver image ads for the keywords you've selected. In this case, CrispAds will deliver appropriate text ads instead, and you'll collect the standard $.20 per click.

One small but clear advantage CrispAds has over AdSense is that they're willing to send payment for any amount over $5, as opposed to AdSense's $100 minimum. This will be helpful for bloggers who are just getting started and would really like to make use of that $95 sitting in their accounts. CrispAds pays on or before the seventh of every month. If your balance is less than $500, CrispAds pays only to a PayPal account. If you balance exceeds $500, you have the option of collecting payment via PayPal or check. For more information about CrispAds, visit their website at www.crispads.com.

Pheedo

Pheedo is another blog-specific advertising network. It offers text ads through CPC and what they call flat-rate campaigns. They have no minimum traffic requirements, so you can sign up as soon as you get started blogging, and like CrispAds, they don't use automated keyword crawlers to determine what ads are placed on your site.

Unlike CrispAds, however, you don't select individual keywords to determine which ads are displayed. Instead, you choose the ads themselves to display. This has the same drawbacks of CrispAds' method but goes even farther toward ensuring that irrelevant ads are never shown on your site.

Pheedo pays 65 percent of all advertising revenue that your site generates for Pheedo. This means that the amount per click you earn is variable and dependent on how much the advertiser pays Pheedo per click. This could mean either huge revenues or a pittance, depending on the ads you select.

Pheedo pays every 30 days, via PayPal or check, to all account holders who have accumulated a balance of $1 or more. This means you'll have no more need to anxiously watch the mail slot for those $101 checks. For more information about Pheedo's services, visit http://site.pheedo.com.

Wait, You Still Have More Choices

There are too many ad networks available to bloggers to cover them all in detail. Beyond the standards already described, there are still many to be explored, with even more features and innovations.

Here is a list of some other advertising networks you might want to research:

- *AdGenta:* www.adgenta.com
- *Adknowledge:* www.adknowledge.com
- *Bidvertiser:* www.bidvertiser.com
- *Clicksor:* www.clicksor.com
- Google *DoubleClick:* www.google.com/doubleclick
- *Marchex:* www.industrybrains.com
- *Miva:* www.miva.com
- *PeakClick:* www.peakclick.com
- *RevenuePilot:* www.revenuepilot.com
- *Text Link Ads:* www.text-link-ads.com
- *TextAds:* www.textads.biz
- *Tribal Fusion:* www.tribalfusion.com
- *ValueClick Media:* www.valueclickmedia.com
- *Vibrant:* www.vibrantmedia.com
- *YesAdvertising:* www.yesadvertising.com

Private Sponsors

The most profitable blogs use private sponsors/advertisers instead of, or in addition to, their other revenue streams. This is where the big money lives, and it will be entirely up to you to go out and get it, provided you have a massive audience that's appealing to advertisers.

By cutting out the middleperson when it comes to ad sales, you keep 100 percent of the revenue you generate. You're no longer depending on other services to provide your profits, and you no longer need to stick to their policies and payment schedules. Remember, this is your business. You're offering a valuable service to both your readers and your advertisers. You should have a say in how, when, and how much it will cost to connect those two groups.

> **Smart Tip**
> Soliciting a sponsor for your blog lets you maintain much more control than running ads for products and services you have *no* control over, plus you can set your sponsorship rates based on the size of the highly targeted audience you can deliver.

The problem is, you need to do the work. You can read here how to go about it, but unfortunately, only you can make the phone calls, prepare the materials, sell the ad space, and invoice the advertisers. As a blogger, obtaining private sponsorships should be your goal. It will take some time for you to build your blog traffic, credibility, and professionalism to a point where advertisers will take your blog seriously. Use the alternative methods above until you really get rolling. Then begin to research possible companies that might be interested in striking a deal with you. You'll hear a lot of rejections, but the affirmatives will make it worth it.

The Media Kit

In order to sell advertising on your own, you'll need to specify and quantify exactly what it is that you're selling. This information takes shape in your blog's media kit. This document is vital for selling ad space to businesses/advertisers. It presents all the data that businesses (potential advertisers) need to know about your blog, audience, traffic, and what you offer.

Describe Your Blog

The first part of your media kit—your blog description—is the easy part. In this first section, you should simply describe your blog and the topics it covers. Provide some background information about why you started the blog, company milestones, and any awards or honors you've received along the way. Present yourself as a company, not as a blogger.

Audience

The next section, your audience, is a little bit trickier to compile, and it will take a fair amount of research. Advertising businesses need to know exactly who their ads are reaching. They won't spend a penny with you if you can't prove that you have a targeted audience for their product or service. So it's in your best interest to collect all the information you can about the people who come to your blog.

To collect information, you'll need to perform a survey of your readers. This data will need to be as unbiased as possible and draw from multiple cross-sections of your readers.

Here are some factors that businesses will be looking to learn.

- *Age.* Age ranges are preferable. Presenting just the average age of your readers doesn't provide advertisers with much useful information. It's more useful for them to know, for example, that 18 percent of your readers are between the ages of 18 and 25, 60 percent are between the ages of 26 and 35, and 10 percent are between the ages of 36 to 49.
- *Gender.* Percentage of male vs. female followers.
- *Location.* If you have a largely international audience, ask for countries. If most of your readers are from the United States, collect state data. The more specific your data, the better.
- *Education level.* How educated are your readers/followers? Are they high school or college graduates, or do they hold advanced or higher level degrees?
- *Occupation.* Occupational industries are preferable to user-supplied data. Everyone has a different title, and learning that some of your readers are "Consultants" isn't helpful. Instead use categories like education, manufacturing, health care, communications, finance, retail, food service, etc.
- *Annual salary.* What's the average income of your readers/followers?
- *Time spent online.* How much time does your average reader/follower spend online or reading your blog? The more you know about their daily habits, the better.
- *Role in purchasing at work.* This tells the advertisers if there's a potential business market among your audience. If they can advertise to business decision-makers using your blog, this is something they'll want to know.
- *Type of personal spending.* This data is important because it describes where your audience's personal discretionary spending goes. Businesses will use this factor to decide whether or not advertising on your blog will be effective. Again, use categories, such as technology, sporting goods, media entertainment, etc.
- *Number of children, if any.* Advertisers want to know if your audience contains parents. Parents are a market unto themselves. Bachelors tend not to buy diapers, minivans, or pacifiers.
- *Size of household.* The number of people in any given household clues advertisers in to the number of people your targeted audience has influence over.

These questions are just a few examples. But keep in mind that your blog's readers won't want to sit through a 30-minute survey. If you have more questions than you can

These Services Make It Easy to Add Surveys to Your Blog

If you want to quickly and easily add surveys to your blog, which in turn should help to boost engagement, here are a few survey companies to consider:

- SurveyMonkey: www.surveymonkey.com
- Vista Online Surveys: www.vista-survey.com
- QuestionPro: www.questionpro.com
- SurveyGold: www.surveygoldsolutions.com
- Verint: www.verint.com
- Zoomerang: www.zoomerang.com

squeeze into a reasonable amount of time, separate the questions and perform multiple surveys over the course of several months.

There are several ways to perform a survey. For example, you could enlist the help of a professional survey company. Collecting 50,000 surveys, analyzing the data, and pulling it all together in some sort of cohesive form is a Herculean task. It will take up all your time and drive you crazy. These services have tools specifically designed to perform this task and can do more, more effectively, than any individual could with years to prepare.

Once you have your data collected, you should put it together in an easily readable, attractive format.

Traffic Level and Analysis Services

Now that you've established what your blog is, and who the people are in your audience, it is time to show how often your audience shows up. The third section of your media kit is devoted to your traffic levels.

Your site should have all along been automatically collecting more traffic data than you can ever hope to understand. This is a standard feature with most third-party web hosting services, but if you host your own server, or if you use a web-based blogging service, you might need to enlist the aid of a traffic reporting service. These traffic reporting services simply monitor all the traffic that comes to your site and keeps records about who's visiting, from where, at what times, and for what content. If presented correctly, this can be extremely helpful and interesting information.

Just a few services that offer website traffic analysis services and tools include:

- *Google Analytics* (www.google.com/analytics/). Use the free Google Analytics service to learn which of your online marketing initiatives are cost effective and determine how visitors actually interact with your site. Make informed blog design improvements, drive targeted traffic, and increase your conversions and profits based on your discoveries.
- *iWebTrack* (www.iwebtrack.com). For a low monthly fee (which depends on which package you purchase), this service offers a variety of traffic monitoring and reporting tools. A free 30-day trial is offered.
- *SiteTrafficStats* (www.sitetrafficstats.com). This service has a $29.95 annual fee and offers the ability to generate a handful of different website traffic-related reports.
- *StatCounter* (http://statcounter.com). This is a free service that provides a website hit counter and basic traffic analysis tools. Upgraded, fee-based tools are also offered.
- GoDaddy's *Site Analytics* (www.godaddy.com). For a low, flat fee per month, GoDaddy.com offers a comprehensive website traffic reporting tool that provides a variety of different reports about who's visiting your website or blog.
- *VisiStat* (www.visistat.com): Available for about $30 per month, VisiStat contains all the tools and reports necessary to monitor your blog's visitors, optimize your online presence, follow marketing, and increase your return on investment. VisiStat can be a problem-solver for blogs, small-business sites, and even the largest multidomain enterprises.

Once you've compiled a few months' worth of traffic reporting, you should include it in your media kit in an easy-to-access format. Use charts and graphs, with full color. You should include such traffic statistics as overall page impressions per day/week/month, unique visitors per day/week/month, average time visitors spend on your blog, average number of pages viewed by visitors per visit, hourly usage, usage on days of the week, and anything else you deem appropriate for potential advertisers to know.

If you have statistics about how your ads from other sources have performed, include those numbers as well—conversion and click-through rates, impressions per month, and so on.

The Offer

The final piece of your media kit is your offer. This is a summary of what you've displayed in the previous pages and what exactly you're offering to the advertiser, and at what price. Remember, you're selling a service here. You set the price and the deliverables.

In defining your deliverables, detail how many ads you'll show per page and in which high-traffic locations. Make it clear how many ads you expect will be shown over the course of a month. In setting a price, bloggers usually use the CPM pricing method. Set a price per thousand ads shown and offer an upper limit to the client in case your monthly traffic levels go through the roof. Another, and easier, option is to offer a set price for a month for advertising, independent of traffic levels.

If you decide to sell advertising space on a per-month basis, take orders well in advance of when you need to. Book space for August in April if you can. This will give you plenty of time to coordinate ads, graphics, and payment before it's time to switch over all the ads on your blog. Hopefully this schedule will give you an opportunity to book September, December, and so on, before you're stuck with a month with no private sponsor.

Whatever payment method you choose, CPM or monthly, have a contract prepared and ready to sign. The advertiser will likely take the time to look it over and make suggestions, but have it ready for them to do so. A fair and common payment schedule to include in the contract for this type of monthly advertising is 50 percent of the contract upfront to secure the spot in your schedule and 50 percent at the month's end. Taking half payment upfront provides a nice cash cushion, which makes budgeting easier. Be prepared to negotiate with prospective advertisers. Most advertisers know not to pay the rates listed on any rate card or price sheet.

Your ultimate goal should be to enlist private sponsors as clients of your blog and use them in addition to some ad network advertising, while at the same time doing a little merchandising and possibly some memberships. You'll need to test each of these methods, then tweak them for maximum profits. Some methods won't succeed on your particular blog, and that's OK. Dump them and move on, because other methods *will* provide you with the profits you're looking for. Don't linger on what isn't working.

Tip...

Smart Tip

Be open to negotiation, but go into the meeting with potential advertisers knowing your bottom limit. You don't want to sell advertising space on your blog to private sponsors if you can make more with that space using the CPC and CPM ad networks.

Running Multiple Blogs

Once you get your blog up and running, evaluate whether or not it's producing the income you'd like it to. If it's not, you'll need to do some troubleshooting. If you find that your blog is running as smoothly and as profitably as it can, and it still isn't producing the profits you'd like, you may have reached the upper limit of what your chosen topic can earn. If this is the case, don't fret.

Beware!

Only start a second or third blog if you have the time or the resources to do so without crippling your main blog.

Remember, there are only so many blog readers available at a given time (though this number is currently skyrocketing), and that means that your chosen topic may have a profit ceiling. Many of the most successful bloggers maintain blogs with limited earnings. They overcome one blog's stagnation by starting another. Running two, three, or 20 blogs is not uncommon in the world of professional blogging. It's much easier to create three blogs that earn $2,000 each per month than it is to create one that earns $6,000. This is because each blog will have a different audience with untapped resources.

If you're faced with a blog with slowing growth and profits, starting a second blog may be an option. But don't be too quick to start an additional blog until you've exhausted the possibilities of maximizing the first. Check your post quality, look for new competition, do more marketing, and then, if that doesn't work, start that second blog that you've been thinking about.

It may be necessary to begin hiring help, or soliciting the help of contributors to keep more than one blog producing reliably at the same time. Evaluate your time. Search for areas of your workday that might be easily left to somebody else. Filling that position could free you up to devote your attention elsewhere.

5

Transitioning from a Hobbyist into a Professional Business

When you reach the point where your blog has grown from a fun hobby into a moneymaking venture, if you haven't already done so, you'll need to transition yourself into a fully fledged business operator, which means filing paperwork with local, state, and federal authorities, including the IRS.

In order to go about operating a business, including hiring employees, opening a business checking account, accepting credit cards with a merchant account, and so on, it's critical that you set up a business entity and legally register your business. Also, setting up your blogging business with the government can provide you with some legal and tax protections, and benefits. For example, as a business operator (professional blogger), you become eligible for various tax deductions, and your blogging equipment (such as your computer, internet service, and cell phone charges) becomes deductible.

If you need help deciding which business model is best for you, consider speaking with an attorney and/or an accountant (CPA). You'll want to understand the legal and financial benefits (and drawbacks) of each business type, and how your personal, professional, and financial life will be impacted, before choosing which type of business to operate.

Business Classifications

For tax purposes, you'll need to define your new blogging business to the IRS. There are several types of business classifications to choose from, each with benefits and drawbacks. Choose the one that best suits your blogging ambitions and your overall business goals.

> Tip...
>
> **Smart Tip**
>
> Before you can open a business checking account or credit card merchant account, you must register your business's trade name with your state government.

Sole Proprietorship

A sole proprietorship is the most common type of startup business. Setting it up requires very little paperwork and few costs. This type of business is applicable if you're the only owner. Legally, financially, and tax-wise there's no difference between you and your business. Your business's assets are your assets. Your business debt becomes your personal debt. And, your business's profits are your income (which must be declared to the IRS).

The advantage to this type of business is that it's easy to start, and you keep all the profits for yourself. You need only to file a business income form (Schedule C), along with your regular state and federal taxes. The disadvantage of this type of business is that you're personally liable for all the business's debt and mistakes. If your blog is sued for any reason, you're directly sued and personally held responsible.

Partnership

A partnership is similar to a sole proprietorship, except instead of one proprietor, there are two. Both parties are legally and financially responsible for the business. Some partnerships are based on common interests (such as a husband-wife team), and some are based on financial need (such as the financier/investor and the business operator/founder).

If you're interested in setting up a partnership, be sure to be excruciatingly clear going into the business about who takes on what role, who makes what decisions, and who receives what money. A clearly defined relationship will go a long way toward making the business relationship a success.

In a partnership, it's important to understand that both parties (the partners) are equally responsible for the business's debt and/or if the business is sued, for example. Neither a sole proprietorship nor a partnership offers the legal protections that a corporation enjoys.

Corporation

Unlike a sole proprietorship or partnership, a corporation is its own legal entity. A corporation's debt, taxes, profits, and legal liability are separate from the corporate owner(s). This provides immense legal and financial protections for the business owner(s); however, corporations can be tricky and expensive to get started.

Most startups don't immediately become a corporation. However, based on the scope of your blogging business, your attorney and/or accountant may deem it a wise business strategy to establish a corporation right from the start.

If you're interested in starting a corporation, you should contact an attorney in your area for help, although there are various services you can use to set up a corporation quickly and for less money than if you hire an attorney, assuming you have a full understanding of the incorporation process.

Legal Zoom (www.legalzoom.com/business-formations/business-formations.html) is just one of many options for establishing a corporation yourself, using an automated online process. The cost is as little as $139.

Tip...

Smart Tip

The U.S. Small Business Administration (SBA) offers extensive online information for small-business operators, including professional bloggers, that covers how to incorporate a business and whether incorporating is actually necessary. Visit www.sba.gov/content/how-do-i-incorporate-my-business.

S Corporation

An S corporation provides tax benefits to owners. Instead of taxing owners twice, like corporations do (once as corporate income tax and once on owner dividends), an S Corporation doesn't pay taxes on its corporate income. Owners only pay taxes on their own income from the S corporation.

S corporations offer all the same legal and financial protections that corporations do, so this may be a smarter choice for your blogging business. Again, check with an attorney or accountant for help in determining what will work best for you, based on your business goals, finances, and the scope of your blog(s).

Limited Liability Corporation

Like an S corporation, limited liability corporations (LLCs) provide owners with legal and financial protection, while avoiding the double taxation that occurs with corporations. This is quickly becoming the default choice for small businesses—and a smart choice for self-publishers, such as professional bloggers. If you publish any sort of material that could be considered libelous, you should definitely protect your personal assets by setting up an LLC.

Setting up an LLC is relatively easy and inexpensive. Any lawyer, accountant, or online-based incorporation service will be able to assist you in quickly establishing an LLC.

> **Dollar Stretcher**
>
> To save money filing the necessary paperwork to establish your legal business entity, you can take a do-it-yourself approach using a service such as LegalZoom (www.legalzoom.com). It's important, however, to first consult with an expert to determine what type of business entity you should establish, and then make sure you fill out the appropriate forms based on the state where the business is being established.

Registering Your Business Name

In many states, it's necessary for you to register your business name, sometimes called a "fictitious name," with the state before you can do things such as open a business bank account or apply for a bank loan. If you intend on asking your advertisers to make out their checks to a business name (and you should), you'll be required to register that business name with the state.

Registering your business name also ensures that you have the rights to that name in your state. Other companies will still be able to operate under the same name, but if it ever came to a legal battle, you would have a claim. Registration is an easy process that involves a simple form, a small processing fee, and a stamp. Check with your state's Small Business Association website for more information.

> **Smart Tip**
>
> With local branches nationwide, SCORE is a volunteer organization that's dedicated to helping new businesses learn and grow. Visit www.score.org for more information.

If your company name is unique or made up, you'll definitely want to protect it by registering it as a trademark and/or copyrighting the name. This involves two different processes. Copyrighting a name is easy and requires that you fill out a form (and pay a small fee). Registering a trademark for a unique company name and logo is a bit more complicated. Any lawyer will be able to help you with this process, although it's definitely something you can do yourself with a bit of research.

For free information about registering copyrights and to download the appropriate forms, visit www.copyright.gov. The U.S. Patent and Trademark Office (www.uspto.gov) is the place to turn to for information about registering a trademark.

Hiring Help

Up until this point, if you've operated your business as a sole proprietorship, you haven't needed an Employer Identification Number (EIN). An EIN is to a business what a Social Security number is to an individual. It simply identifies your business to the IRS, and is used when you withhold income taxes from your employee's paychecks.

You must receive an EIN before you begin hiring part-time or full-time employees. To apply for your EIN, fill out and submit IRS Form SS-4. It can be downloaded from www.irs.gov/pub/irs-pdf/fss4.pdf.

When you hire new employees, in addition to keeping their application, resume (if submitted), and references on file, you also need to collect some tax information from them. As the employer, you'll be withholding income tax from your employees' paychecks (unless they're hired as independent contractors or consultants). The amount you withhold is determined by the information your employees fill out on their Form W-4. You'll need to keep a copy of Form W-4, and mail one to the IRS.

You must also ask your new employee to fill out Form I-9, the *Employment Eligibility Verification*. To do this, you'll need a copy of the employee's passport, or driver's license and Social Security card. For a complete list of acceptable forms of identification, see the back of Form I-9. You must keep every employee's Form I-9 on file for a period of three years from the hiring date.

As soon as you're ready to start hiring employees, have a discussion with your accountant to make sure all the paperwork is completed and filed correctly.

Initially, however, you can hire freelancers, independent contractors, and consultants to help you on a part-time basis, without having to do the majority of the paperwork needed when hiring actual employees. The paperwork required for hiring freelancers, independent contractors, and consultants is greatly reduced.

If you need help finding freelance writers (blog contributors), editors, photographers, graphic designers, illustrators, web page (blog) designers, programmers, or any other type of help, you can find highly skilled, experienced, and talented individuals advertising on services like CraigsList.org, eLance.com, Freelance.com, and Guru.com. Hiring independent contractors (freelancers) is done on a work-for-hire basis. In other words, these people are not your employees. If you hire a freelancer, however, make sure you have something in writing that states you own the copyright to all work created for your blog.

When it comes to promoting your blog, you might want to solicit the help of freelance public relations professionals, advertising specialists, or SEO experts, since generating hype about a new blog is a skill unto itself and one that requires experience, time to implement, and tremendous creativity.

Smart Tip

Many businesses secure an EIN number long before it's time to hire employees. In addition to its main tax purposes, it can be a handy identification number for your business if you're concerned about revealing your personal Social Security number when establishing business relationships with vendors, banks, etc.

As the employer, try to hire freelancers on a per-project basis, instead of at an hourly rate. For writers and editors, you'll probably wind up negotiating a per-word rate. Before hiring anyone, ask to see samples of their work as well as a resume. Depending on what you're hiring the freelancer, independent contractor, or consultant to do, you could also ask them for references.

More Protection

To further protect yourself, your business, and your blog's original and proprietary content, be sure to register your blog with the U.S. Copyright Office as a periodical. (This is in addition to copyrighting your original company or blog name.)

Copyrighting your entire blog will protect your content legally so in the event that you find a renegade blogger copying your posts, and therefore, stealing your original and valuable content, you'll already have established legal ownership of your content. If you don't have your copyright, you're often without legal recourse.

Text, videos, photos, original graphics, multimedia animations, and other blog content can all be copyrighted. At the very least, you should display appropriate legal-lingo on your blog that relates to copyrights.

Include a message on the main page of your blog that reads:

> *[Insert Blog Name] ©2013 [Insert Blogger's Name]. All rights reserved. No portion of this blog, including any text, photographs, and artwork, may be reproduced or copied without written permission.*

There is a small registration fee and a few forms to fill out when filing a copyright, however, the process takes just a few minutes to complete. After the appropriate forms are submitted and processed, you'll receive your certificate of copyright within several months; however, your copyright protection begins on the date of the postmark when you filed the copyright. Find out more at www.copyright.gov/register/serial.html.

Tip...

Smart Tip

If you have a unique logo for your blog (which is recommended), seriously consider registering it as a trademark, especially if you plan on doing any merchandising. Visit the U.S. Patent and Trademark Office (USPTO) website for more information at www.uspto.gov.

Play by the Rules

As a blogger within the United States, you are covered by the U.S. Constitution and have freedom of speech to say just about anything within your blog. However, you must adhere to the content guidelines issued by your blog hosting platform, and you are not allowed to violate the copyrights or trademarks owned by others.

So, before plagiarizing text, using digital images (photos) that don't belong to you, or incorporating art, music, sound effects, logos, graphics, or other content that you don't own, either obtain written permission from the copyright or trademark owner, or avoid adding this content to your blog or vlog.

At the same time, as you're creating content, be mindful that you need to adhere to laws pertaining to slander, invasion of privacy, and identity theft, for example. Violating any of these laws could result in you being sued and having to pay thousands of dollars in fines or damages.

Beyond what's permissible by law, however, consider your own online reputation and credibility. If you develop a reputation for including inaccurate, fraudulent, offensive, or otherwise distasteful content within your blog, you run the risk of quickly alienating your audience.

As a general rule, as a professional blogger (or a blogger whose blog represents a company or organization), avoid content that may be considered controversial, discriminatory, racist, or that could tarnish your blog's reputation, or whatever organization you're representing.

6

Meet Established Bloggers and Learn from Their Success

In this chapter, you'll meet a few established and successful bloggers and learn from their firsthand experiences. What you'll discover is that the bloggers featured in this book are everyday people who have a passion about a particular topic and who have become experts about that topic.

By combining what they enjoy with some hard work, they've managed to create blogs that now attract vast audiences, and in some cases, have generated enough revenue to allow them to quit their day job.

Liz Corry, Blogger, MySubscriptionAddiction.com

Liz Corry, 28, had a somewhat unique hobby. She became obsessed with subscription boxes. In order to reach out to other subscription box enthusiasts and share her knowledge, she created a blog that reviews and discusses them. Within about one year, her blog, called *My Subscription Addiction*, now receives nearly one million page views per month and is growing rapidly.

In recent years, subscription boxes have become a popular way for consumers to sample a variety of new products every month that relate to a specific interest or product category.

For example, for $19 per month, subscribers to Bark Box (www.barkbox.com) receive a box in the mail each month that contains a different collection of sample dog toys, treats, and other unique pet-related products (often from smaller companies that don't yet have national distribution). Subscribers get to learn about and try new dog products, without having to find and then purchase the full-priced, full-size version of the product since in many cases, only sample trial sizes of the products are provided.

One alluring aspect to subscription boxes for consumers is that a typical box contains products that are worth a much higher dollar value than what the subscriber actually pays. To appeal to a wide range of people, companies have begun offering subscription boxes relating to all sorts of product categories, from gourmet foods, teas and coffees, to cosmetics, grooming products, dog products, and items of interest to moms, babies, kids, brides and bridesmaids.

In this interview, Liz Corry talks about how she transformed a passion for subscription boxes into a successful part-time blog that now allows her to generate an income each month that's significantly higher than what she earns doing her full-time job.

How did you become a blogger?

Liz Corry: I am employed full time by a large ecommerce company as a product manager, so I have knowledge about the internet. However, I never really thought of myself as an aspiring blogger. Just over a year ago, I discovered subscription boxes and became absolutely obsessed with them. I kept going online looking for new subscription boxes to subscribe to, but found it difficult to find the information I was looking for online.

I decided to create a blog that's dedicated to reviewing every single subscription box that's available to consumers. So basically, my blog started because I was searching for something on Google, could not find what I was looking for, and decided to create something that provided others with subscription box information in one centralized place.

Once you decided to create a blog, how did you decide which blogging platform to utilize?

Corry: My first mistake was starting the blog using Blogger.com and relying on the generic domain name that I was provided with. At that point, I had no idea if anyone else would be interested in my blog idea, so I didn't invest too much time and effort into buying a domain name or researching blogging platforms. Once I discovered that people were interested in my blog, and month after month I saw my traffic dramatically increasing, I realized that I needed to get serious about managing the blog, so I registered the www.MySubscriptionAddiction.com domain name, and I made the switch to WordPress. I now use the free WordPress installed server application and have GoDaddy.com hosting the blog.

If you expect to get a lot of traffic from search engines, you need to host your blog using WordPress. Once I made the switch, my traffic almost immediately tripled as a result of having the blog indexed with the major search engines faster and more accurately, thanks to WordPress. The way WordPress is built, it is easier, apparently, for search engines to crawl through entries, pinpoint keywords, and index blog entries. The more and more posts I add to my blog now, the more I see traffic increase as a result of search engine traffic.

Compared to Blogger.com, did you find WordPress to be more difficult to use?

Corry: Yes, WordPress is definitely a bit more complicated to use, but it's also much more powerful. For someone with no website design, website management, or programming experience whatsoever, I recommend starting a blog using an easy-to-use service, like Blogger.com. WordPress has more of a learning curve to get it set up and working correctly, but once you get the blog designed exactly how you want it, the day-to-day management of the blog is very easy with WordPress.

If you do opt to use WordPress, I recommend hiring a freelance website designer to help you initially design and set up the blog, plus customize the template, for example. Then, as a non-tech-savvy blogger, you can learn to use the WordPress blogging platform using the various online tutorials available.

As you first started blogging, what were some of the mistakes you made that you needed to overcome?

Corry: My blog is review based. I have three basic categories of posts. I review subscription boxes and offer photos of them, but also include news about new boxes and details about coupons or promotions related to boxes. Initially, I had to pay for all of the subscriptions myself, out of pocket, and that started to get very expensive. In order to save money, I tried to reach out to subscription box companies asking for free samples, but I did this too soon, before my blog was established, and they didn't take me seriously. I didn't yet have enough traffic.

Also, when I did try to make contact with the subscription box companies, I used a generic Yahoo! email account, so I lacked credibility, since the emails didn't appear to be coming from a legitimate business. Today, I have an email address [liz@mysubscriptionaddiction.com] that relates directly to my blogging business.

As a new blogger, make sure you're established before you reach out to companies, and once you do, make sure you approach them in a professional and credible way that shows you're serious about what you do and that you have a large and growing audience.

In just over one year, your blog has built up an audience of more than one million views per month. How did you achieve this while maintaining a full-time job that's not related to your blog?

Corry: The vast majority of my first-time visitors come from the search engines. The search for subscription boxes is a fast-growing trend right now, and if you do a search for "subscription boxes," "subscription box reviews," or "subscription boxes for women," for example, using one of the major search engines, a listing for my blog pops up as one of the top three search results.

As I write each blog entry, I am always thinking about how I can optimize my blog using keywords, tags, and descriptive titles, for example, to make the blog post more SEO friendly.

The other thing I've done to build my audience is to embrace every online social network that I can and that works well for what I do. Pinterest is a useful tool for me, for example, because my blog features a lot of photos that are taken primarily using my iPhone's camera.

Another thing that drives significant traffic to my blog is the "Share" button that appears as part of each post. This allows readers to share details about a post with their friends via email or one of the popular online social networks with a single mouse click. Word-of-mouth among subscription box enthusiasts has been very beneficial to me and my blog's popularity.

Having a short, opt-in daily newsletter that gets emailed to my subscribers, and that highlights new additions to the blog, also helps to generate repeat traffic and keep subscription box enthusiasts coming back to my blog for the most up-to-date information. The newsletter serves as a daily reminder for people to come back to the blog and see what's new.

When I first started my blog, one thing I did that worked very well to build traffic was to be a guest blogger on other blogs, for free. In exchange for creating content for those other blogs, my posts included a direct link to my blog. This helped to spread the word about *My Subscription Addiction* and to establish me as a leading expert about subscription boxes.

Bloggers are always looking for new and fresh content, so becoming a guest blogger to other blogs was relatively easy and mutually beneficial for me and the other bloggers.

Has running MySubscriptionAddiction.com become a full-time job for you?

Corry: Right now, I still maintain my preexisting full-time job and operate the *My Subscription Addiction* blog during my free time. I dedicate three to four hours per day running the blog. However, it's gotten to the point now where I am making more money off of my blog than I earn at my full-time job, so I am definitely thinking about making a career change and becoming a full-time blogger.

Blogging does take more time than I initially anticipated. In addition to constantly creating new blog content, it takes time to respond to comments and emails, and also to continuously promote the blog by staying active on all of the online social networks, for example. It also takes time to do basic maintenance on the blog and constantly go back and update older blog entries to keep them current.

I try to update the blog three to four times per day. I have discovered that on the days when I am more consistent posting multiple entries and they're spread out throughout the day, my daily traffic numbers tend to be better. My goal is to offer something new to dedicated readers every time they come back to the site.

I have discovered a handful of ways to make certain tasks more automated in order to save me time as a blogger. For example, there's a widget I use with WordPress that automatically publishes details about new posts to all of the online social networks that I'm active on. Plus, if I share an image on Instagram, I have a tool that automatically shares that same image on Twitter, Tumblr, Pinterest, and Facebook as well.

Have you used any paid online advertising to promote your blog?

Corry: When I first launched the blog and signed up for Google Analytics, I was given a free $100 credit to use Google AdWords. I tried running ads using that service, but the $100 ad budget was used up in less than one day, so I quickly discovered that wasn't something I could afford to maintain.

What has worked very well for me is running online giveaways in conjunction with the various subscription box companies. These giveaways are promoted on their websites and through my blog, and require participants to share details about my blog with their online friends via online social media. As a result, these giveaways generate new traffic to the blog in multiple ways, plus they enhance the ways existing readers interact with the blog. Running giveaways is also free for me as the blogger.

To run many of the giveaways through my blog, I use a service called RaffleCopter [www.rafflecopter.com]. It is powerful, flexible, and easy to use. It also offers the most flexibility and options for both the blogger and the people participating in the giveaways.

What tips about keeping content fresh can you offer to a first-time blogger?

Corry: For me to keep up the pace of four to five posts per day, I create a stockpile of posts and then schedule them out. There is a widget for WordPress that allows you to create and upload drafts of multiple posts, and then plug them into a calendar so they're published automatically on the day and time you as the blogger pre-select.

This allows me to see the big picture for an entire week of the blog's editorial calendar and determine when and where new content should appear. Seeing this big picture helps me make sure the blog isn't too review heavy on certain days, and it keeps me from accidentally focusing on one type of subscription box too much in a single week. For example, I don't want to put too much emphasis just on baby products or cosmetics.

Planning ahead eliminates the need for me to scramble at the last minute to just get new posts published, without putting enough thought into them and how each post fits into the rest of the blog. Planning also helps to eliminate stress related to blogging.

Another trick I have learned that works very well when I don't have ideas for fresh content is to repackage older content in list form. For example, I'll create a blog entry based around a top-five or top-ten list, such as "'The Five Best Subscription Boxes for Teens." These lists are very SEO friendly and offer a new take on older content. Whenever I do create a list-type post, I always link back to the original posts about each product on the list. This, too, helps build traffic to older entries, plus is SEO friendly.

When adding a link back to an older post, instead of saying something like, "Click here to view the post about . . .," I discovered it's much more SEO friendly to include the title of the other post within the text, not just the words "click here."

Do you have any design tips for the basic layout and design for a blog?

Corry: When bloggers first start including ad banners within their blog in order to earn money, they think that by displaying a ton of different banners, it will increase their revenue. I have found that this isn't the case at all. I have had much better luck limiting the number of ads displayed on the screen. This makes my blog's layout look much cleaner, better showcases the ads, and as a result, the response to those ads is much higher.

If you're working with an affiliate program and have access to hundreds of different banner ads you can put up on your site, be very selective and limit yourself to very few ads that you think will have the most direct interest to your audience. There is a growing trend of "banner blindness" among [internet users]. If you have too many ads displayed on a screen, people just ignore all of them.

I also recommend refreshing banners regularly and making sure that all of the ads are displayed using the same banner size. Again, this helps convey a clean, well-designed site that's easy on the eyes and that's clutter free.

If you will be using a lot of images within your blog, originally, I was uploading the full-size images and then resizing them within WordPress. By doing this, the blog was loading the full-size image and then resizing them each time a page was loaded, and this slows down loading time and hurts performance times. Since performance time also impacts search engine rankings, I recommend pre-sizing images before uploading them to WordPress.

Also, choose a consistent size to display all of your images. This is yet another way you can achieve a clean, clutter-free blog from a design standpoint. You don't need to be a graphic designer to set your own style guide for your blog, but whatever you do decide on, make sure you use that design consistently. Don't change the layout, color scheme, or design elements for each of your posts. Consistency is important for building a professional reputation.

What color scheme, fonts, and typestyles you use, for example, are a matter of personal taste. My personal preference is to have a clean and well-organized appearance for my blog that uses a simple background and the same font throughout the site. As a background, you can't go wrong using solid white. If you opt to use a designed background, make sure it doesn't distract the reader, take away from your blog's professional appearance, or make your content more difficult to read on the screen. Make sure your blog is easy to read.

Have you adopted a special writing style for your blog?

Corry: No. I have been writing as myself, providing the information that I myself would want to obtain from the blog. I use my own voice and try to convey my own personality.

You mentioned you're now generating a significant income from your blog. How exactly are you achieving this?

Corry: It's a result of a combination of things. I use Google AdSense to display ads on the site because the ads that appear automatically target the customers, based on the content that appears within each blog entry and on each page of the blog. This is one source of revenue for me.

However, my main source of income on the site is affiliate sales. These links appear within the posts themselves, not necessarily as ads. If I am reviewing a subscription box, I will include an affiliate link for that box that a reader can use to subscribe to it directly from my blog. If a reader purchases that subscription box, I receive either a percentage of the ongoing sale or a one-time fee.

How have you seen blogs evolve in recent times, and how do you see blogging evolving in the future?

Corry: My blog is designed to be responsive. No matter what screen size someone is using to access my blog, the content will automatically format for that size screen, even if it's a tablet or smartphone. I think this is extremely important, since more and more [internet users] and blog readers are using their mobile devices to access and read blogs. This is a trend that I see growing in the future.

I also pay careful attention to up-and-coming online social networking sites and try to build up my user base on these emerging services quickly. In the past year, for example, I have seen the popularity of Google+ and Vine grow dramatically among my target audience.

In the next few years, I know blogging will evolve as the technologies change. I am seeing YouTube vlogging becoming extremely popular right now, but at the same time, I think there will always be a place for traditional text and image-based blogs. Also, thanks to the growing popularity of Pinterest and Instagram, for example, publishing high-quality images is becoming increasingly more important. I think the importance of incorporating images into a blog and using digital images in conjunction with the online social networking sites will continue to become more and more important.

Over the next few years, I think there will be major changes in online advertising and in how affiliate programs operate. Based on this assumption, I am trying to diversify as much as possible and not rely on any single source of advertising revenue.

For you, what is the most rewarding aspect of blogging?

Corry: Initially, it was receiving my very first comment. At the time, I didn't know if people were really reading my blog and taking it seriously, so when I started receiving comments, that was a very important validation for me. Later, another milestone was when I received my first check from Google AdSense. It was only for a few dollars, but it proved to me that I could make money doing this.

Overall what I am rewarded by is the feedback I get from my readers, the fact that I am blogging about something I am passionate about, and that I am now earning a really good salary by doing something I love.

Is there any additional advice you'd like to share?

Corry: I think it's absolutely essential that you blog about something you're passionate about. Developing and maintaining a successful blog takes a lot of work and dedication. If you're not passionate about what you're doing, every aspect of running the blog will become a tedious chore, and that won't help you achieve success or maintain your level of excitement or creativity.

Don't choose a blogging topic just because you think you'll make a lot of money doing it. During those first few months of blogging, you are probably not going to make any money. Thus, staying motivated during that time will be difficult if all you care about is the paycheck.

Also, before launching your blog, figure out what competition you have in the blogosphere and on the web in general, and figure out how you'll do things better or approach the topic from a unique angle. Finally, be consistent with your approach to blogging and your content. My readers know what to expect when they read my blog, and I think that's very important.

Micah Warren, Blogger, OffTheRecordSports.com

Micah Warren, 35, is a sports enthusiast. He loves all aspects of sports, including sharing his opinions and commentary about the topic. In 2008, he began blogging about his passion, and over time, has developed a vast audience of dedicated followers.

While Micah does earn a small income from blogging, he does it as a hobby and enjoys the other nonmonetary perks that are associated with being a successful sports blogger, including access to well-known professional athletes, the ability to attend team practices and media days, as well as receiving free tickets or media credentials to attend games and sporting events.

How and why did you become a blogger?

Micah Warren: I am a huge sports junkie. Back in 2007, I used to regularly read a blog written by a sports radio host in Philadelphia. At one point, this blogger decided to switch to a paid subscription-based model. I decided to email this guy and tell him how bad an idea that was.

Out of the blue, this sportscaster whom I idolized called me and we had a long discussion about what would make his blog successful. During that discussion, I also brought up the idea of me contributing to his blog. I emailed him a few samples, and he later invited me to write for his site. That's how I got started doing sports blogging. Eventually, I developed my own following.

After I established myself on that blog, I reached out to an online magazine, called *Blast*, and recommended that they start a sports section. This led to several conversations with the publisher that resulted in me being hired in an unpaid position to be the publication's sports writer. That was back in 2008, and it was how the first iteration of *Off The Record* came into being.

As I was writing for *Blast*, I noticed there were ads on the site and it was generating money, but I was not being paid. This was when I decided to launch my own independent blog, called *Off The Record Sports* [www.OffTheRecordSports.com].

What are some of the things you've done to drive traffic to your blog?

Warren: I have utilized a service called Google News [http://news.google.com], and have made it so my blog appears on that site. This has generated a tremendous amount of traffic for me. In one instance, as a result of a blog post appearing on Google News, I was invited to be a guest on a major sports radio show, which also helped to boost my credibility and audience.

Another thing I have done to drive traffic to my blog is to be active when it comes to reading other people's blogs and posting constructive or relevant comments. In conjunction with my comments, I somehow incorporate my blog's URL. In addition to directly driving traffic to my blog, this also creates more backlinks to my blog which helps with SEO. Google and other search engines like to see backlinks, and commenting on other people's sites and blogs is a great way to create them, while making yourself known within the community you're blogging about.

Tip...

Smart Tip

Information about how to submit your blog and content to Google News can be found at http://support.google.com/news/publisher/bin/answer.py?hl=en&answer=40787.

What platform do you use to host and manage your blog?

Warren: WordPress. I can't emphasize that enough. In my opinion, and after doing extensive research, WordPress is by far the best blogging platform out there. Search engines love WordPress.

There are several plugs-ins you can use with WordPress to help with SEO, including Yoast SEO [http://yoast.com/wordpress/seo] and All-In-One SEO Pack [http://wordpress.org/extend/plugins/all-in-one-seo-pack] and both are really, really powerful.

WordPress is infinitely customizable, even if you're not a coder. There is also a vast selection of optional plug-ins, widgets, and templates that allow anyone to quickly and easily add functionality to a WordPress blog . . . using a cut-and-paste or drag-and-drop process.

How large is your blog's audience?

Warren: I am up to 50,000 unique visitors per month. A lot of my audience comes from search engines. As I am creating content for my blog, I am very conscious about making it SEO friendly. One way I do this is to carefully choose SEO-friendly titles for each blog post. I also use descriptive and relevant file names for all of my images, so for example, the images show up on Google Images and Yahoo! Images.

There was one time when I equated something having to do with Britney Spears with the sports topic I was writing about. It was meant to be a joke. However, because the photo of Britney Spears I used was properly named, it wound up being listed within Google Images, and it drove an additional 10,000 people to my blog.

What advice can you offer about writing compelling content for a blog?

Warren: As a blogger, you do not have to write Shakespeare-quality work every day. For my blog, I follow the sports news. I determine what's happened, recap the news story, and then provide my commentary about it. I keep my topics timely and I keep my posts short and to the point. People don't access a blog to read novel-length posts. They want to gather information quickly and easily.

As a blogger, don't try to make blogging a bigger task than it has to be. It doesn't have to be difficult or a burden. Figure out what people want to read and what interests them, and then provide that.

Are you very active on various online social networking sites?

Warren: Yes, but until you build a following on these sites, they won't help you too much in building a large audience for your blog. These services are useful, however, once you have a following and want to tell those people about new posts on your blog or other information relating to it. Initially, instead of focusing on using Facebook and Twitter to promote your blog, invest your time becoming consistent, publishing posts and content to your blog.

Blogging is like taking care of a plant. Just as you have to water a plant every day, you have to spend time every day updating and caring for your blog, or else people will stop caring about it and it won't grow. A successful blog is all about content. You need to create and publish content continuously, even on days when you're not in the mood to do it.

Do you have any tips for monetizing a blog?

Warren: This has not been a primary goal for me; however, I recommend that a blogger become familiar with ad networks and affiliate networks. Learn how they work and discover how you can incorporate ads from them into your blog, based on your target audience and what your goals are for the blog.

Getting involved with an ad network or affiliate network is very easy and it can be done quickly. Then, as the blogger, all you need to do is cut and paste a few lines of code into your blog in order to make content-appropriate ads appear, for which you have the opportunity to generate revenue.

Don't even think of going out and trying to sell ads directly to advertisers on your own, unless you have a dedicated and consistent audience in the hundreds of thousands or millions of active readers per month. Even then, you'll have better results working through an agency which specialized in this.

What tips can you offer on how to make a blog successful?

Warren: Do not start blogging for the money! It takes time to build a blog and you'll become discouraged long before your blog starts to generate revenue. For me, I am a sports junky and it's my passion for sports that keeps me going. I love writing about athletes and sports, and sharing my sense of humor about this topic with others.

For you, what are the biggest perks of being a well-established sports blogger?

Warren: Through my blog, I put all of my thoughts about sports in one place, so I don't have to have the same discussions over and over with my friends who want to discuss last night's game. I also love being a guest on sports radio shows, which has become a pretty regular occurrence. Running this blog does not pay my mortgage, but it does provide plenty of beer money. Another perk is getting to meet and interact with athletes and getting media passes to all sorts of events and games, including NFL training camps. It's a dream come true for me, plus it provides more inspiration for the blog's content.

How much time do you spend working on your blog each week?

Warren: At least five hours per week. A lot depends on what's happening in sports and what inspires me to create posts.

Since starting your blog, what were some of the biggest mistakes you've made and how did you overcome them?

Warren: There have been a few times when I got away from offering opinion-related content within the blog and I was too heavy on news. My goal is not to compete with ESPN.com. People don't read my blog for sports news. They want my commentary. Maintaining focus and consistency within a blog is essential.

When I am stuck about what to blog about, I always come up with a list. People love lists.

Another thing to remember is that if you make some type of major change to your site, go back and make sure everything still works. Double- and triple-check everything, including all links and the placement of images and other content. It's very easy to make a change and have something go wrong that you don't notice initially, but it impacts your blog's traffic dramatically because something isn't working correctly.

In terms of a blog's design and layout, do you have any tips to share?

Warren: As far as designing the blog, remember that people will be reading your blog for the content. However, you want to make sure everything is easy to read, pleasing to the eye, and well organized. The flashiest and most visually impressive site in the world is irrelevant if people have no interest in your content and what you have to say or share.

Come up with a design and layout that you like and that's appropriate, but focus on your content. In terms of templates you can use to customize your blog, there's a website called ThemeForest.net that offers more than 9,400 different website and blog designs that are sorted by category and topic relevancy. They're very affordable.

In terms of a blog's readability, go with a white background with black print. That's the easiest to read. People try to be creative and use a black background with white text, for example, and that's very difficult to read. Make your content easy to read. You can always use a fancy background to frame your text, for example, but keep the text itself simple—white background with black print, and choose an easy-to-read font.

You can also use photos to break up your text, as long as you own the rights to the images and you name them appropriately. When adding an image, name the file, add a caption, and add a description for each image to make it SEO friendly.

How do you think blogs will evolve in the future?

Warren: I think mobile devices will play an even bigger role in how people access and read blogs. Thus, I think the revenue model for mobile content will change dramatically, since there isn't a widely successful way to monetize mobile content yet. I think Facebook will play a huge role in developing ways to monetize mobile advertising. From the blogger's standpoint, I think the tools for blogging and creating content from a mobile device will become even more powerful. Right now, I rely on the WordPress app on my phone to create and publish posts remotely.

In the past few years, I think blogging has had a huge influence on mainstream media. Today, bloggers are breaking major news stories and have become as credible, and in some cases more credible, than some major news organizations.

While bloggers technically do not need to follow the same rules as journalists, in reality, they do. That is, if they want to earn credibility and respectability, and maintain their readership. Bloggers who are successful need to establish themselves as a trusted source of information for whatever they're blogging about.

Janet Barclay, Blogger and Blogging Consultant, www.OrganizedAssistant.com

As a small-business operator, Janet Barclay discovered she had a flare for blogging back in 2006, when she decided to create and manage a blog as a marketing tool for her professional organizing service business. The results were better than she anticipated.

Today, Janet Barclay has a sub-business working as a paid blogging consultant to other professional organizers. She helps them to create, publish, and establish their own blogs to be used as marketing tools for their respective businesses.

How do you describe what you do?

Janet Barclay: I am a WordPress professional virtual assistant who specializes in helping professional organizers to maximize their online presence through blogging.

In other words, I do everything from WordPress theme design and customization to helping people brainstorm ideas to blog about. I also help with the day-to-day editing and proofreading of my clients' posts, and occasionally do some ghost writing as well. My various clients have different needs, but all of my clients are professional organizers.

Why did you decide to specialize in WordPress?

Barclay: WordPress is the blogging platform I learned first. I really like it because it's easy to work with and the support that's available is phenomenal. There are also many plug-ins, widgets, and themes that make this blogging platform extremely customizable and versatile. I typically work with the installed server edition of WordPress, as opposed to WordPress.com, because it has a lot more capabilities for customization.

How do you stay informed about all of the latest WordPress-related developments?

Barclay: Within WordPress, I work exclusively within the Builder Responsive Multi-Purpose Theme [http://themeforest.net/item/builder-responsive-multipurpose-theme/3596009]. This provides a general structure for a blog. I can then choose from more than 80 themes that work with Builder, and can customize any of them.

Every theme within WordPress works differently. Instead of having to learn how to use every theme that's out there, and there are thousands of them, I have narrowed my focus and work with the WordPress Builder theme exclusively.

In your opinion, what goes into creating a really awesome blog?

Barclay: The visual appeal of a blog is huge. I also make sure that the blogs I work with all link to the popular social media services. In terms of creating compelling content, people want to read short, but highly informative or entertaining posts. Readers don't want to read long essays. Their attention span is short and the blogger needs to accommodate for that.

If you want to have an occasional longer post, that's fine, but the average person should be able to read a post and digest its content in less than three minutes. When I am working on a post, I always try to draw the reader to read additional posts on the blog as well, and try to lure them into becoming a subscriber, for example. Once someone accesses your blog initially, you want to get them to keep coming back.

Always try to end a post with a call to action. This might include posing a question that the reader can answer in the form of a comment. A call to action might also be to get the reader to share the post they're reading by clicking on a "Share" button, or to subscribe to your blog by clicking on a "Subscribe" button.

One of the best pieces of feedback I ever received from a reader was a comment that said, "I read your blog, and I felt like you were talking directly to me." As a blogger, this is the best type of feedback you should strive to get, because it's proof you're communicating effectively and engaging your readers.

In terms of a blog's layout and design, do you have any tips to share?

Barclay: Try to make your blog look unique. However, avoid using a color scheme that makes the blog difficult to read. Avoid lots of animations or bright colors that will annoy or distract the reader.

In terms of the font, select one primary font to use for your posts and then stick to using just that font. Don't change fonts for each post. Maintain consistency. You can, however, do something a bit fancier with post headings.

To help ensure each post is SEO friendly, as you're writing, focus on using appropriate and relevant keywords in the post itself, as well as within your titles and tags. If necessary, use the Google Keywords Tool [www.googlekeywordtool.com] to help you compose a list of keywords you can use within each blog post, based on the popularity of keywords being used on Google.

As you're writing, there's a difference between utilizing SEO-friendly keywords and over-using them to the point that it becomes annoying for your readers.

What are some of the biggest mistakes you see bloggers make on a consistent basis?

Barclay: One thing that really bothers me is when bloggers are sloppy. They may have some pretty amazing ideas to share, but their grammar is sloppy, so their posts are painful to read. Some people use the excuse "It's just a blog" to justify this laziness, but poor grammar and punctuation, as well as lots of misspellings or misused words within a post, make it very difficult to read.

Also, watch the tone of your blog. If you're trying to promote a business, product, or service, it's very easy to be too sales-oriented within a post. This is a huge mistake. Provide valuable information to your readers via your blog, and utilize your company's website to be a strong sales tool. A blog should be used to take a soft-sell approach.

Another mistake I see often is that bloggers solicit comments, but then when they get them, the comments are ignored. If you receive comments, as the blogger, you need to respond to them in a timely manner. Also, be diligent about deleting spam comments.

What do you think is the biggest misconception people have about blogging?

Barclay: If you build it, they will come. Many people create a blog, publish a few posts, and then move on with their lives. They're ultimately disillusioned by the low level of traffic their blog receives. This leads to the erroneous conclusion that blogging doesn't work.

The reality is that blogging takes a lot of work and it's something you need to keep up over the long term. A blog is also something you need to actively promote on an ongoing basis. Once you stop promoting your blog, you will see the traffic to it dwindle.

I always recommend to my clients that they should update their blog with new content at least several times per month, or if possible, much more frequently. If you're using a blog to promote a business, for example, allow it to showcase your expertise and experience, based on the content you publish.

What should people do to promote their new blog?

Barclay: Take advantage of email to tell the people you know about the blog. Also, promote the blog using all of the online social media channels that are relevant to you and your business, such as Facebook, Twitter, Google+, and LinkedIn. I also suggest getting your blog listed with the popular blog directories. Most important, focus on SEO and make sure your blog's content is SEO friendly.

Christina Zila, Blogger and Executive with Textbroker International, www.textbroker.com

Textbroker International was established in 2008 to provide bloggers with all of the content creation services they need to develop and maintain a successful blog. To accomplish this task, the company works with thousands of well-established and highly skilled writers from around the world. In this interview, Christina Zila, an executive with the company and an experienced blogger herself, shares some advice about content creation.

What is Textbroker International and how does the company work?

Christina Zila: We are an online-based content creation company. In other words, we offer writers for hire. We write anything from blog posts and articles to product descriptions, catalog copy, or any other text or content that our clients require. We cater to many different types of clients, from independent bloggers who need help creating posts, to small, medium, and large size businesses and corporations.

For a blogger, we serve as a really nice backup resource. A blogger can order content when they need to go on vacation, get sick, or they become overwhelmed with other tasks. In this situation, we can help the blogger brainstorm ideas for posts, or create content based on ideas generated by the blogger. Even for the smallest independent blogger, our services are extremely affordable and we offer fast turnaround time for the work we do. Our services are priced by the word, and our prices start at $0.02 per word.

What advice do you have for people first launching a blog?

Zila: Textbroker expects its clients to know what type of content they want, understand who their audience is, and already have the voice and tone established for their blog. Then, we can step in and help brainstorm ideas for posts and/or create actual content for a blog.

We have discovered that the best results come about for a blog when the blogger really knows and understands their audience. The blogger needs to see things from their audience's point of view and provide content that caters to the wants and needs of their audience. One way to get to know your audience is to become active and interact with them using the various online social media services.

After you determine what your audience wants or needs, you need to figure out how you, as the blogger, will interact with your audience and convey the information you want or need to share. It's basically an exercise in branding. As a blogger, you need to brand yourself and your blog, know your voice, and know your topic.

What do you believe are some of the benefits to becoming a blogger?

Zila: We have seen many of the successful bloggers who hire us leverage their popularity as a blogger to get hired for paid speaking engagements. Thus, they're able to generate revenue as a speaker as well as a blogger. In these cases, some of our clients use Textbroker International to generate blog content while they go off traveling and speaking.

What advice do you have about keeping blog posts short and compelling?

Zila: Research shows that longer and more in-depth blog posts generate more engagement and social interaction. This only works, however, if the subject or topic you're writing about deserves a long-form post. The drawback is that many people lose interest in long-form posts due to their short attention spans. Thus, your longer posts may appeal to a smaller audience, but those people will potentially become more engaged within your content.

Instead of using lots of words to convey information, consider using photos, charts, tables, graphics, and lists whenever possible. We have found that a typical blog post works well if it's around 500 words. Of course, this varies a lot based on the topic and the intended audience.

A good blogger knows in advance what the purpose of their blog is and what specific message they want to impart on their readers with each post. The blogger should also know what they want the reader to do immediately after reading a post. Should the reader be laughing? Should they take a specific action, like read another post? If an action is required, the blog post should include a detailed and easy-to-understand call to action.

I believe that all blog post ideas have some merit. The question the blogger needs to address is whether or not each idea they come up with deserves its own post, or if it should become part of another post. Again, this decision should be based on the target audience and what the blogger is trying to accomplish.

What other tips do you have about creating compelling content?

Zila: If your blog will represent a company, one of the best things you can do with it is to use it as a tool to personify your business. Many companies want to position themselves as big corporate entities. However, consumers like to buy from people who are like them, and they're more likely to make purchases from people, not companies, that they relate to.

Companies can use a blog to establish a personal connection with their customers and build that all-important psychological connection with them in an informal, yet professional way. Many companies have a very impersonal or corporate reputation and mentality that a blog can be used to modify in order to achieve better business results.

When creating blog content, transparency is essential. Don't misrepresent yourself or your organization using false or misleading information. This is the fastest and easiest way to lose your credibility as a blogger. As a blogger, it's important to fact-check, disclose, and be transparent, just like a mainstream journalist.

How do you see blogging as a whole evolving over the next few years?

Zila: I think we're already seeing more and more people using mobile devices, particularly tablets, to access blogs. I believe this trend will continue and it will dramatically impact how, when, and where people consume information and access their favorite blogs. These mobile devices will allow people to access blogs away from their computer, so what people read in blogs will become more of a conversation starter than ever before.

7

Final Thoughts

You now have the basic tools and the know-how to start your own blogging business or a blog that represents your company or organization in a positive way. After reading this book, you should understand what you need to accomplish to jump-start your professional blogging career.

Remember, blogging is a quickly evolving phenomenon. It's essential that once you get started that you stay on top of the latest trends and blogging technologies in order to meet or exceed the expectations of your target audience.

As you continue to develop new and innovative content for your blog, be sure to keep reading and researching, not just about your chosen topic or subject matter, but about the latest trends and happenings within the blogosphere.

> Tip...
>
> **Smart Tip**
>
> While it costs practically nothing to launch a blog, if you want it to be successful, plan on spending considerable time creating original content, analyzing and getting to know your audience, and then heavily promoting your blog on an ongoing basis.

If you learned nothing else from this book, here's a quick summary of the most important ideas you need to comprehend before launching your blogging career and venture.

Six Strategies for Improving Your Blog

The following are basic blogging strategies that every professional blogger should implement to help ensure success:

1. Define the Target Audience for Your Blog and Cater to That Audience

The best way to build a dedicated audience for any blog is to carefully and clearly define its target audience right from the start, and then create content that caters to that audience.

Focusing on a niche audience and developing appropriate content specifically for those people helps to ensure there will be a strong interest in your blog's content, plus it makes promoting the blog easier.

The more narrowly you define your target audience, the easier it will be to identify those people, cater to their needs with your content, and reach them with your advertising and marketing messages.

The target market or audience you identify for your online content can be defined using one or multiple criteria, or various demographic characteristics, such as:

- Age

- Club memberships
- Education
- Geographic area
- Hobbies
- Income level
- Marital status
- Occupation
- Religion
- Sex
- Sexual orientation
- Special interests

Reaching a niche audience or target demographic on the web is relatively easy (much simpler than doing it using traditional advertising practices in the real world). Carefully designing your online marketing efforts to appeal to your target audience will help you set yourself apart from your competition and pique the interest of internet users who are inherently interested in what online content you're offering.

2. Put a Unique Twist on Your Blog's Topic and Content

It's virtually impossible to brainstorm a totally original topic to blog about. Instead, your primary and ongoing goal should be to continuously develop innovative content and to put a truly unique twist or spin on whatever topic you're blogging about.

You, as a blogger, are a unique individual with your own personality. To set your blog apart, be sure to incorporate your knowledge, voice, and personality into your blog. This is one of the easiest ways to set it apart from your competition.

You can also set your blog apart, for example, by including proprietary information, publishing extremely timely facts or research, or by incorporating your own unique thoughts, ideas, perspective, or expertise into each of your blog entries.

Be sure to research how other bloggers and website operators are presenting similar information, and then develop innovative ways to do it better or in a more unique, attention-getting, and memorable way. Even after your blog is operational, you'll want to keep constant tabs on what your competition is doing, plus stay up-to-date on trends happening within the blogosphere.

Another important strategy for creating and publishing a successful blog is to develop content that isn't readily available elsewhere in the blogosphere or on the

> **Beware!**
>
> Simply republishing content from other blogs, RSS feeds, press releases, websites, or other published content, then relying on keyword optimization to generate traffic, won't allow you to create a successful blog with long-lasting appeal. While you can use some of this content, it's essential that you also offer original and unique content that caters to your audience.

web. (Or in any other form of media, for that matter.) The more unique and innovative your content is, and the better you target your audience, the easier it will be to build up a vast following.

3. Add New Content on a Regular Basis

Launching an interesting, informative, entertaining, or otherwise cutting-edge blog is the first step. However, to build and then maintain a steady (and ever-growing) audience, regularly add new content to the blog. Every new blog entry should cater to the blog's target audience, offer content that's perceived as valuable, and build upon previously published content.

For any blog to be successful, the blogger must always stay on topic and cater to the wants, needs, and expectations of the target audience. This means developing a thorough understanding of who your audience is comprised of, then adjusting your focus as trends and demands change over time.

Once you set a schedule for posting new content, it's essential that you maintain that schedule, so plan accordingly and don't be over-ambitious. You're better off promising new content once a week then posting twice or three times per week on occasion, as opposed to promising new content daily (or several times daily) and not being able to deliver.

4. Focus on Engagement: Transform Your Blog into an Interactive Online Community

Instead of focusing exclusively on publishing content for your blog's readers, develop your blog into an interactive online community. Encourage your audience to post feedback and comments, interact with each other, share their ideas, and enhance your content by adding their own information. It is, however, the blogger's responsibility to moderate this audience interaction prior to it being published in order to ensure relevance.

Also, be sure to incorporate a "Share" button into each of your blog entries. Make it very easy for your readers to share your content with their friends via email, Facebook,

Tip...

Smart Tip

By allowing your readers and followers to voice their own opinions and post comments, for example, you're creating a simple but effective interactive community around your blog. This is a great way to build loyalty.

Google+, Twitter, or LinkedIn, for example. Virtually all of the popular blogging platforms offer a widget that makes it very easy to integrate a "Share" button into your blog. Doing this can help you build your audience through virtual word-of-mouth.

5. Adopt a Multifaceted Approach to Promoting Your Blog Continuously

It will take weeks, possibly months or even years for a blog to build an audience in the hundreds of thousands or millions. To achieve this level of success will typically require ongoing marketing, promotions, and even paid advertising. Many of the world's most successful bloggers have relied on the mainstream media to generate publicity for their blog to help build an audience. Even after your blog is successfully launched, promoting it on an ongoing basis is as important as regularly adding new content.

6. Keep the Blog's Look, Overall Design, and Content Professional

As you create your blog and its content, focus on conveying a professional image, regardless of the subject matter or your audience. The look and overall design of your blog should be professional, and easy to read and understand.

Also, be sure to edit and proofread your work carefully to avoid or correct errors, typos, and misspellings. Spelling mistakes or grammatical errors in your blog take away from your credibility and make your blog appear amateurish.

If you're not good at editing your own work, consider hiring a freelance editor to review your content before it gets published online.

Tip...

Smart Tip

As a general rule, the simpler your blog's layout and design, the better. Make sure your blog is visually appealing, and easy to read and navigate. Use white space on the screen to your advantage, and avoid clutter. Distracting graphics, color schemes, or animations, for example, are a no-no.

Additional Things to Consider

Throughout your blogging experience, keep the following strategies in mind in order to help keep you on track, focused, and providing content that will interest your readers and followers:

- While starting a blog is an inexpensive process that anyone can do with relative ease, it will take a considerable amount of time and creativity to develop truly unique, original, innovative, informative, educational, and/or entertaining content on an ongoing basis. Make sure you are up to the challenge and have the time to invest.
- Just because you publish a blog doesn't mean it will immediately develop a massive following. To generate an audience for your blog, you'll need to heavily promote your online venture using a wide range of different methods that are carefully targeted to your blog's audience.
- It's important to have very realistic expectations and understand that, depending on how you promote your blog, it could easily take months or even years before your blog builds an audience in the thousands or millions. Be persistent and patient.
- Keep in mind that people are impatient and busy. If you want readers to become loyal to your blog and follow it regularly, offer the content they want in a format that's quick and easy for them to access. Keep your blogs relatively short and to the point. If you're vlogging, keep new posts well under 10 minutes in length.

Take Advantage of Technology to Help You Blog

As a blogger, you're no longer tied to your desktop computer when it comes to creating and publishing content. To make your life easier as a blogger, consider investing in a tablet, such as the Apple iPad, and then installing a specialized blogging app that's been designed to work in conjunction with your blogging platform. For example, free apps are available to maintain a Blogger.com or WordPress blog.

Using one of these apps allows you to create and publish blog content virtually anytime and anywhere inspiration hits you. Also, take advantage of the camera that's built into your smartphone or tablet to capture images, as appropriate, that can be incorporated into your blog with ease.

There are also widgets you can add to your blog that allow you to automatically publish details about your latest posts to your Facebook page, Twitter feed, Google+ account, and to the other online social networking sites you're active on. Setting up this feature will help you promote your blog without having to invest any additional time to post details about new blog posts on each individual online social networking service.

Also, many blogging platforms allow you to upload new posts in advance and then schedule exactly when they'll be published. So, if you need to take time off from your blog to go on vacation, for example, you can create your blog posts for that period ahead of time and have those posts automatically published on the days and times you specify.

This type of scheduling tool can also be used to plan your editorial calendar and determine what topics you'll want to blog about and when. (Of course, you can also use a traditional calendar or even a dry erase board.) Often, when planning future blog posts, looking at the big picture will help you group together related posts, avoid repetition, and brainstorm new approaches to take with your content.

One Last Thought . . .

It will be the next generation of bloggers, of which you are one, who realize the full potential of blogging. Be ambitious. Be creative. Be innovative. But, most important, have fun!

Glossary

Archive (noun): The area of a blog where old posts are stored and indexed, yet still made available to the blog's readers.

Bleg (verb): To use one's blog to beg for assistance (usually for information, occasionally for money). One who does so is a "blegger." Usually intended as humorous.

Blog Hosting Service (noun): These are online-based services that offer the tools and resources needed to create, publish, manage, and promote a blog, without having to install any type of specialized software onto a computer. The tools offered by these services are web-based, and the blog content created is hosted by the service (also referred to as a Hosted Blog Service).

Blog Publishing (verb): The act of posting blog content to a blog and making it available to the online public.

Blogathy (noun): When you just don't give a damn about posting no content to your blog on any given day.

Blogger (noun): Someone who creates, manages, and publishes a blog.

Blogger.com (noun): A free, online-based blog hosting service that's operated by Google. It's one of the most powerful and popular blogging tools available to bloggers.

Blogging (verb): The act of creating and publishing blog entries to be posted to a blog.

Blogorrhea (noun): An unusually high-volume output of articles or new content on a blog.

Blogosphere (noun): When someone refers to cyberspace in reference to where all of the millions of blogs can be found, it's referred to as the blogosphere.

Blogroll (noun): A collection of links to other blogs. When present, blogrolls are often found on the front page sidebar of most blogs.

Comment: A blog comment is feedback from a blog's reader to a particular blog entry that is usually posted for the public and the blogger to read. When a blogger requests that readers "Comment on the blog," they're requesting that readers (or viewers if it's a vlog), post their feedback. Most blogging applications and blog hosting services offer the ability for blog readers to post their feedback in the form of comments.

Content (noun): The text, photos, video clips, graphics, artwork, audio, and other multimedia assets used to create blog entries and populate a blog.

CPC—Cost Per Click (noun): When it comes to online-based advertising, this is a method by which advertisers pay to have their ad displayed online. A fee is paid only when a web surfer actively clicks on an ad, not each time the ad is displayed and seen by web surfers.

CPM—Cost Per Thousand (noun): When it comes to online-based advertising, this is a method by which the advertiser pays a pre-set fee per 1,000 people who see an ad that's displayed online, regardless of whether the web surfers click on or respond to the ad.

CSS (noun): An acronym for Cascading Style Sheet.

Flame (verb): To flame someone is to make a hostile intemperate remark, usually of a personal nature.

Keyword (noun): A word or phrase used within online ads, blog content, or within other online content to help search engines properly organize, index, and list online-based content by topic.

Micro-Blog (noun): Made popular by Twitter, this is a form of short-form, text-based blogging that requires the blogger to create just one sentence for each blog entry (usually limited to just 140 characters). Some micro-blogging services allow photos or website links (URLs) to be incorporated into a micro-blog post.

Mobile Blogging (verb): The act of creating blog entries using a cell phone, wireless PDA, or other mobile device. Apple's iPhone, for example, has dozens of apps available to bloggers that can be used for creating, publishing, and managing blog content and entire blogs while on the go.

Niche Audience (noun): This is a carefully defined audience for a blog or vlog. A niche audience can be based on age, sex, religion, occupation, geography, income, interests, or anything that helps to define a narrow demographic.

Online Social Network (noun): Services like Facebook, MySpace, Twitter, LinkedIn, and others are referred to as Online Social Networking sites, because they allow everyday web surfers to communicate, exchange ideas, publish, and read member-created content, and interact within an established online community.

Permalink (noun): A link to a specific article in the archives of a blog, which will remain valid after the article is no longer listed on the blog's front page (i.e., after it has been archived).

Ping (noun): When used in reference to blogs, the act of sending electronic, usually automated, notice of a blog's recent update.

Pingback (noun): A method for web authors to request notification when somebody links to one of their documents.

Podcasting (verb): To record (usually spoken narrative) audio files (usually in MP3 format) and make them available online so that they can be downloaded and listened to rather like an "on-demand" radio show.

Post (noun): A blog or internet forum entry.

Poster (noun): Someone who posts an entry to a blog.

RDF (noun): RDF is a web content syndication format. Acronym stands for Resource Description Framework.

RSS Feed (noun): RSS is a family of web feed formats, specified in XML and used for web syndication.

Search Engine (noun): An online directory, such as Google or Yahoo!, that allows a web surfer to enter in a search word or phrase and find online content that directly relates to what they're looking for.

Search Engine Advertising/Marketing (noun): A paid opportunity for advertisers to display short, text-based ads on search engines (and affiliated content) that is keyword based, so the ads are seen by a very targeted audience.

Search Engine Optimization/SEO (noun): Steps used to help ensure a website or blog, for example, receives a prominent listing on a search engine, thus increasing the chances that a web surfer will visit the site or blog.

Spambot (noun): Online code that automatically generates large numbers of unwanted messages and directs them at members of the public. Within the context of blogging, it is code which enters unsolicited comment spam.

Target Audience (noun): The intended audience for a blog, as defined by the blogger.

Thread (noun): A series of remarks posted by people in a public comment section of a blog that follow a conversational and topic-related sequence.

Trackback (noun): A mechanism for communication between blogs.

Traffic (noun): Refers to the number of people who read a blog or watch a vlog. The size of a blog's audience. A blog's traffic can be analyzed by the blogger to help him/her determine who is reading their content, where they're from, and when the content is accessed.

Tweet (noun): An individual micro-blog entry is called a Tweet when it's published on the Twitter service. In 140 characters or less, the Tweeter can answer the question, "What's Happening?"

Twitter (noun): Currently the largest micro-blogging service in existence. The service is free to use. People enjoy using Twitter because they can manage their Twitter Feed from any computer, cell phone, or PDA that's connected to the internet. Thus, it's possible to Tweet from almost anywhere, anytime.

Twitter Feed (noun): When someone uses Twitter to post a series of Tweets on an ongoing basis, it's referred to as their Twitter feed.

Vlog (noun): Video blog. A blog used to display various forms of video images or video-based blog content.

Vlogger (noun): Someone who produces, records, manages, and publishes a video-based blog (also referred to as a vlog).

Vlogging (verb): The act of recording, producing, and publishing a video-based blog entry (also referred to as a vlog).

Wiki (noun): A type of collaborative online software that allows readers to add content on a subject, which can also be edited by others (for example, Wikipedia).

XML (noun): A web language used for (among other things) syndication formats used on blogs. Acronym for eXtensible Markup Language.

XML Link: Text or an image on a blog that has been linked to the blog's RSS feed.

YouTube: The premier site for publishing and distributing video content, such as vlogs, on the internet. YouTube is a free service.

About the Author

Jason R. Rich (www.JasonRich.com) is the bestselling author of more than 55 books that cover a wide range of topics. He's also a frequent contributor to numerous national magazines, major daily newspapers, and popular websites and is an accomplished photographer.

Of interest to bloggers, some of Jason's books include: *Ultimate Guide to YouTube for Business* (Entrepreneur Press), *Blogging for Fame and Fortune* (Entrepreneur Press), *Click Starts: Design and Launch an Online eCommerce Business in a Week* (Entrepreneur Press), and *The Unofficial Guide to Starting a Business Online* (Wiley).

Some of his other recently published books include: *Your iPad at Work* (Que), *iPad and iPhone Tips and Tricks* (Que), *How to Do Everything iPhone 5* (McGraw-Hill), *How to Do Everything MacBook Air* (McGraw-Hill), and *How to Do Everything iCloud* (McGraw-Hill).

If you're an Apple iPhone or iPad user, you can read more than 130 how-to articles that are part of an ongoing series written by Jason R. Rich and published on the Que Publishing website (www.iOSarticles.com).

Jason R. Rich lives in Foxboro, Massachusetts. In addition to maintaining his own blog (www.FeaturedAppOfTheWeek.com), you can follow him on Twitter (@JasonRich7).

Additional Books Written by Jason R. Rich and Published by Entrepreneur Press

The following books are now available wherever books are sold, or can be ordered from EntrepreneurPress.com, Amazon.com, or BN.com. Many are also available in digital form for the Kindle, Nook, and iPad. For more information about these and other books written by bestselling author Jason R. Rich, visit his website at www.JasonRich.com.

The Ultimate Guide to YouTube for Business

Dirty Little Secrets: What the Credit Reporting Agencies Won't Tell You (2nd Edition)

Blogging for Fame & Fortune

Click Starts: Design and Launch an Online eCommerce Business in a Week

Click Starts: Launch Your Online Web Design, Photography, or Graphic Arts Business in One Week

Dirty Little Secrets II: Improving Your Credit Score and Managing Your Mortgage or Refinance

Mac Migration: The Small Business Guide to Switching to the Mac

Smart Debt: Borrow Wisely, Live Rich

202 High-Paying Jobs You Can Land Without a College Degree

202 Things You Can Buy and Sell for Big Profits

Entrepreneur Magazine's Personal Finance Pocket Guides

Buying or Leasing a Car: Without Being Taken for a Ride

Dirty Little Secrets: What the Credit Bureaus Won't Tell You

Get That Raise!

Mortgages & Refinancing: Get the Best Rates

Mutual Funds: A Quick Start Guide

Why Rent? Own Your Dream Home

Entrepreneur Magazine's Business Traveler Series

Entrepreneur Magazine's Business Traveler Guide to Chicago

Entrepreneur Magazine's Business Traveler Guide to Las Vegas

Entrepreneur Magazine's Business Traveler Guide to Los Angeles

Entrepreneur Magazine's Business Traveler Guide to New York City

Entrepreneur Magazine's Business Traveler Guide to Orlando

Entrepreneur Magazine's Business Traveler Guide to Washington, DC

Index

C

D